VICE-ADMIRAL B. B. SCHOFIELD
C.B., C.B.E.

and

LIEUTENANT-COMMANDER (SP) L. F. MARTYN
R.N.V.R.

THE
RESCUE SHIPS

With a Foreword

by

SIR JOHN McNEE
D.S.O., F.R.C.P., D.Sc., F.R.S.(E), M.D.

WILLIAM BLACKWOOD & SONS LTD
Edinburgh and London
1968

0·85158007·6

PRINTED AT THE PRESS OF THE PUBLISHER

WILLIAM BLACKWOOD & SONS LTD, EDINBURGH

SBN: 85158 007 6

*To the Memory of the Officers and Men
of the Rescue Ships who gave
their lives in trying to
save others*

Contents

Chapter		Page
	FOREWORD	xi
	ACKNOWLEDGEMENTS	xvii
	INTRODUCTION	xix
1	WAR AND THE MERCHANT SEAMAN	1
2	THE GROWTH OF THE RESCUE FLEET	17
3	*DE PROFUNDIS*	31
4	ARCTIC ODYSSEY	52
5	RUSSIAN INTERLUDE	70
6	THE COMEBACK	84
7	THOSE INVALUABLE VESSELS	100
8	GADFLIES	121
9	AN EFFICIENT TEAM	137
	EPILOGUE	155

Appendix

I	Nationalities of Survivors	164
II	Details of Rescue Ships, Convoys Escorted and Survivors Rescued	165
III	Convoy Medical Code	166
	INDEX	168

Illustrations

Facing page

Rescue Ship *Rathlin*   12

Boom net and Rescue motorboat   12

Hoisting in a stretcher   13

Rescue Ship *Empire Rest*   13

Transferring men in a basket   44

Artificial respiration   44

A Rescue Ship sick-bay   45

Rescue Ship operating theatre   45

Typical crew members of the Rescue Ships   76

Chief Radio Officer Horace Bell of the *Copeland* and *Zamalek*

Captain O. C. Morris, D.S.O., and the Officers and Crew of Rescue Ship *Zamalek*

Captain L. E. Brown, O.B.E.

Rescue Ship *Bury* arriving Halifax with survivors

Between pages 76-77

Facing page

The survivors of *S.S.Angelina*. The splendid Gustav Alm is in front, wearing a cap   77

Zamalek on arrival at Halifax, Nova Scotia, in January 1943   108

Captain W. G. Hartley, D.S.C.   109

Captain J. L. Davidson with members of *Accrington*'s Ship-Company   109

Captain O. C. Morris, D.S.O.   140

Captain J. M. Haddon, O.B.E., of the *Gothland* with Surgeon Lieutenant J. Mackenzie, R.N.V.R.   140

Captain A. Banning, D.S.O.   141

Rescue Ship at sea with a convoy   141

A 2

Foreword

THE authors of RESCUE SHIPS have honoured me with a request that I should write this Foreword.

The Saga of the Rescue Ship Service in the Second World War should have been written long ago, because of the great interest and importance of what there is to tell and because some similar situation might arise in the future. Practically nothing was known, or could be written, about the Service during the war years, and in fact I believe that the only (much censored) account of the Rescue Ships was written by myself in 1944 and published in the Journal of the Royal Naval Medical Service.* This was to inform at least Naval Medical Officers about what the Rescue Ships were, and what they had accomplished.

My interest in the Rescue Ships was naturally concerned mainly with their medical problems, and a short account is necessary of how it all came about. In 1935, when at University College Hospital, London, I had been appointed Civil Consultant Physician to the Navy. In 1937, when I became Regius Professor of the Practice of Medicine at Glasgow University, my status was changed to Civil Consultant Physician, Royal Navy, Scotland, and I was warned that in the event of war I should have to don naval uniform. Thus in 1939 I suddenly found myself a

---

* *Convoy Rescue Ships.* Journal of the Royal Naval Medical Service, 1945, Vol. XXXI

temporary Surgeon Rear-Admiral with duties including not only Scotland, but the north of England as far south as the Tyne in the east and the Mersey (Liverpool-Western Approaches) in the west.

My first appointment was to H.M.S. *Cochrane* at Rosyth, but when Norway fell to the Germans much of the naval activity in the Forth was quickly transferred to the Clyde. This suited me well and, before long, part of the Gardiner Institute of Medicine of Glasgow University became practically a naval medical office, always in close touch with the main naval office in Glasgow (H.M.S. *Spartiate*) commanded for most of the war by Vice-Admiral Sir James Troup, K.B.E.

I cannot remember how I first heard of the Rescue Ships, but I quickly knew that nearly all the convoys of merchant ships crossing the Atlantic, and later to North Russia, assembled and sailed from Greenock in the Clyde Estuary. I was soon in touch with Lieutenant-Commander L. F. Martyn, R.N.V.R. (one of the authors of this book) who was a member of the staff of the Principal Sea Transport Officer for the Clyde and Scottish ports, and who had been entrusted with the task of organising the newly-conceived Rescue Ship Service. No better choice could have been made, as his previous record and his accomplishments during the war years fully show.

In his young days Martyn covered much of the world in cargo ships and he had the almost unique experience of serving before the mast in the sailing ship *Archibald Russel*. Among his varied adventures, he was shipwrecked in the Solomon Islands. These experiences enabled him to understand the psychology and needs of the merchant seaman. In addition, Martyn belonged to an old established and well-known family of shipbrokers on the Baltic Exchange, London, and thus had considerable first-hand knowledge of the running of ships from the shore end. This was of great value in co-operating with the ship owners whose vessels were taken up for the Rescue Service. As so often happens in war emergencies, Martyn had the task of building up the Rescue Service from practically nothing, with no precedents to guide him and, what is more, single-handed. The results speak for themselves in this book. Little help or encouragement of this new Service came from the Medical Department of the Admiralty, and it was only after pressure from above that naval medical officers (generally young newly-joined R.N.V.R. officers) were appointed to serve in these small converted merchant vessels.

It is unfortunate that no senior medical officer from Headquarters in London ever visited a Rescue Ship to encourage their efforts, although the reports of the young medical officers were regularly available after each exciting voyage. In fact the only naval medical officers in regular touch with the Rescue Ship Service were Surgeon Commander R. S. Rudland, R.N.V.R., of the Glasgow Naval office and myself. It was quite otherwise with the senior naval officers on the Clyde (Sir James Troup and others at Greenock) and on the Mersey (Admirals Sir Percy Noble, Sir Max Horton and others) who knew all the activities of the Rescue Ships and sent many encouraging signals to their Masters, crews, and medical officers.

As stated earlier, not being a sailor I could only hope to help Lieutenant-Commander Martyn and the ships with some of the purely medical problems involved in the rescue work. My many visits to Rescue Ships in port and my discussions with Masters, crews, and (not least) the naval medical officers, were I think greatly appreciated. Occasionally I was able to hasten the delivery of medical apparatus or equipment which was badly needed.

I have always been proud of my association with the Rescue Ship Service, and it therefore gives me great satisfaction that this book has now been written. The nucleus of the book was a moving factual account compiled by Martyn at the end of the war, of which I was given a copy. Many essential documents and reports were, however (because of secrecy at the time) not available to Martyn, so that he could not write this book by himself. Fortunately he got in touch with Vice-Admiral B. B. Schofield, a well-known writer on naval affairs, who was Director of the Trade Division of the Admiralty when the Rescue Service was formed, and who had the knowledge and experience to fill in the details and obtain information not available to Martyn. The result of this collaboration is this splendid, lively and full account of the Rescue Ships and their doings.

Although I was mainly concerned with medical affairs, certain points in connection with the Rescue Ship Service impressed me so deeply at the time that I feel compelled to emphasise them, although they are referred to in the pages of the book :

1. The older type of straight-sided or wall-sided ships were far the best for the efficient working of scrambling nets and boom nets. The frigates provided near the end of the war were much less efficient because of the pronounced flair of their hulls.

2. Ships which, when taken up for service, were already divided into many small compartments or cabins were less suitable than those with simple covered holds. Survivors always preferred to be together in a large space, with easy access to the main deck.

3. The decision to arm the Rescue Ships—they were quite heavily armed for their size—and to fit them with HF/DF radio equipment was thoroughly sound. The effect on morale of young active gunners in action against bombing attacks was tremendous, as I so often heard from survivors.

4. In a few instances the morale of survivors had reached a very low ebb, and the only treatment for the worst cases was an immediate and adequate dose of morphine.

5. All of us closely associated with the Rescue Service were at times much concerned about the transfer of sick or injured members of convoy crews, especially at night and in stormy weather. Was the transfer really necessary ? Was it immediate or could it wait ? Was advice sufficient ? For this reason an abbreviated medical code was worked out by Martyn, Rudland and myself ; it is referred to

in the book, and came into general use in the convoys after long delay. One point about this code, apt to be forgotten, is that it could be easily and correctly used by Masters of Allied merchant ships who had no knowledge of the English language.

JOHN W. McNEE

Acknowledgements

THE authors wish to thank all those who, in one way or another, have contributed to the preparation of the manuscript of this book, and especially those who have lent photographs for reproduction. In particular they acknowledge their indebtedness to : The Clyde Shipping Company, The Dundee, Perth and London Shipping Company, The Institute of Actuaries, Sir John McNee, Kt., D.S.O., F.R.C.P., D.Sc., F.R.S.(E.), M.D., Sir Gilmour Jenkins, K.C.B., K.B.E., M.C., Commander H. Archdale, D.S.C., R.N., Surgeon Commander W. H. C. Hamilton, M.B., B.Ch., M.R.C.S., L.R.C.P., R.N., The Very Reverend the Dean of Battle, F. H. Outram, M.A., Horace Bell, Esquire, Captain Duncan Campbell (former Marine Superintendent of the City Line); Captains L. E. Brown, O.B.E., C. Chestnutt, G. N. Glass, J. Harris, O.B.E. and A. H. Shearer; Doctors G. M. Baird, M.B., B.Ch., M.R.C.P., D.P.M., T. S. Eirmerl, D.S.C., V.R.D., M.D., G. MacBain, D.S.C., M.D., W. H. McCallum, M.B. and R. D. Wilkins, F.R.C.S. ; Mrs C. S. McEuen (formerly of the Ajax Hospitality Group, Halifax, Nova Scotia), and Mrs A. Banning (widow of Captain A. Banning, D.S.O.).

B. B. Schofield
Newholme
Lower Shiplake

L. F. Martyn
Melton Court
Shenfield

Introduction

THE total estimated deaths of officers and men of the British mercantile marine from enemy action during the Second World War is 32,952. To this must be added a considerable number from the crews of Allied merchant ships for whom no figures are available. It is difficult to give an accurate figure for the strength of the British Merchant Navy during the war, but the late Sir William Elderton, K.B.E., Ph.D., F.I.A., who submitted a paper on this subject to the Institute of Actuaries on 25th November 1946, put the figure at between 180,000 and 190,000.* Taking a mean figure of 185,000, the loss rate works out at just over 17 per cent, and this compares with 9.3 per cent for the Royal Navy, 6.0 per cent for the Army, and 9.0 per cent for the Royal Air Force.† Had it not been for the introduction of Rescue Ships with the mercantile convoys, the loss rate in the Merchant Navy would have been even higher. Of the 4,194 survivors rescued by the ships, 2,296 were citizens of the British Commonwealth and 951 of the United States, the balance being made up from the crews of ships belonging to the other Allied nations. (*See* Appendix I.) This, therefore, is the measure of the achievement of the Rescue Ships in statistical terms, but that is not the whole story. The boost which their introduction gave to the morale of the crews of the merchant ships which they accompanied cannot be expressed

* *Merchant Seamen during the War.* Journal of the Institute of Actuaries, Vol. LXXXIII, Part II, No. 337
† *Strength and Casualties of the Armed Forces and Auxiliary Services of the United Kingdom 1939-1945* (Cmd. 6832)

in figures, nor is it possible to count the number of lives saved by the prompt medical attention it was thus possible to provide for those stricken down by illness or injury during voyages ; for a merchant ship (unless it has more than one hundred passengers) does not normally carry a doctor. Finally, the Rescue Ships played an important part in the long drawn-out struggle against the U-boats, not only by virtue of the high frequency direction finding equipment with which they were fitted, but also because of the way in which they were able to relieve the escort commanders of anxiety for the survivors of torpedoed ships and allow them to concentrate their attention on counter-attacking the enemy. But since there were not enough of these ships to enable one of them to be sailed with each convoy, it was necessary to record in March 1943, when the Battle of the Atlantic was at its height, ' No Rescue Ship having been included in the convoy, the escort was at once faced, when the attack developed, with the bitter choice between leaving the survivors from torpedoed ships to their fate, or disorganising and weakening the already inadequate defence.' * All in all, therefore, the story of the Rescue Ships is unique in the annals of maritime warfare. It is one of great humanitarian endeavour, of superb acts of courage, of a display of seamanship of the highest order, of a devotion to duty by medical officers under the most arduous conditions imaginable, of great deeds by men of the Merchant Navy in little ships on voyages they were never designed to undertake.

* *The Battle of the Atlantic,* Donald Macintyre, p. 178

I

War and the Merchant Seaman

IN the battle between the Austrian and Italian fleets off the island of Lissa on 20th July 1866, 900 officers and men of the opposing fleets lost their lives, the greater part by drowning when their ships foundered. This, for those days, heavy number of casualties, aroused the public conscience to the need for action to ameliorate the lot of mariners wounded and ship-wrecked as the result of naval action, and led to the drawing up of rules for the employment of Hospital Ships. These rules were embodied in the Geneva Convention of 1868, and subsequently subscribed to by all the principal powers. They were later included in The Hague Convention of 1907, and remained in force throughout both World Wars, though not observed by Germany in either of them.

The right of a belligerent to capture the merchant shipping of the enemy is well established in international law. At the same time he has a duty, before applying force to capture a ship, to call upon her to stop and submit to a visit. It is also the duty of the captor to take his prize into a port belonging either to his own country or to one of his allies. It is generally accepted that when circumstances make this course impossible of fulfilment, the prize may be destroyed ;

but—and this is the important point—' it is a rule
of international law that all persons on board must
be removed and placed in safety, and that all relevant
ships' papers must also be removed and preserved '.*

When, in 1917, Germany began unrestricted submarine warfare against British and Allied shipping,
she knew it was contrary to the accepted principles
of international law, because the small size of a submarine made it impossible for such a ship to put a
prize crew on board a captured vessel, nor was it
practicable for her to escort the prize into port, let
alone provide accommodation for the passengers and
crew, before sinking her. It should be noted that
ships' lifeboats were not considered places of safety
unless within easy reach of the shore. This new form
of warfare in which ships were torpedoed and sunk
without warning meant that the officers and men of
the Merchant Navy were exposed to dangers similar
to those which members of the armed forces were
expected to face. But while naval officers and men
were trained to fight at sea and to accept the risks
inseparable from their calling, those in the mercantile
marine were not ; they represented a sea-going section of the civilian population, and included in their
number many who were too old or unfit for com-
batant duty, and who could hardly be expected to
face up to the perils of war in the same way as those
in the Services. Submarine warfare struck at a
specially vulnerable part of Britain's defences, and

* *International Law of the Sea.* Higgins and Colombos, 2nd Revised
Edition, 1951. Chapter XX. On the outbreak of the First World War
the German Prize Law contained provisions similar to those quoted
above

it was directed against those least well equipped to withstand it. However, to their lasting credit, the personnel of the Merchant Navy at once showed that they were not to be intimidated in carrying out their vitally important work, but they rightly expected the Government to give them as much protection as possible and to succour them in time of trouble.

A few months after convoy was introduced in 1917, the Vice-Admiral in Charge at Milford Haven recorded his view that ' it was absolutely essential to have a small vessel of some description with each convoy to pick up survivors ', but there is no evidence that the Admiralty took action to comply with this suggestion. Most of the rescue work at that time was carried out by trawlers or other small craft which might happen to be in the vicinity. Twenty years later, when the inevitability of another war with Germany was reluctantly accepted by the British Government, although plans were made by the Admiralty to put shipping into convoy as soon as possible after the outbreak of war, there was still, officially at any rate, a belief that the submarine threat would not be as serious as it had been during the First World War. This belief was partly based on misplaced faith in the efficacy of the Asdic detection apparatus which had been developed between the wars, on the fact that Germany did not possess many submarines, and that she had agreed to abide by the Geneva Convention regarding their use—though few people really believed that she would adhere to it.

In war the Admiralty assumes responsibility for the movements of merchant ships, whether sailing in convoy or independently; but their operation, which includes their ports of call, the loading and discharge of their cargoes, arrangements for bunkers, water and repairs, are all a matter for the Ministry of Shipping, when formed, or, as it later became during the Second World War, the Ministry of War Transport. The equipment carried by merchant ships, apart from their armament and certain items pertaining to convoy which are supplied by the Admiralty, is a matter for the ships' owners in conjunction with the Ministry. This includes lifeboats, rafts, life-jackets — in fact everything considered necessary for saving the lives of the crew should a ship be sunk.

While it is the responsibility of the Admiralty to draw up a schedule of convoys and to arrange for escort vessels to escort them, it is also necessary to lay down the tactics to be employed in the convoys' defence, and to devise an organisation for rescuing the crews of ships which are sunk. Unfortunately neither of these two matters was given full consideration prior to the oubreak of war. Besides the essentially humanitarian aspect of the second of the two duties, there is the need to maintain morale which, as every great leader acknowledges, is of the utmost importance in war. Ships can be replaced in time, but it takes many years to train experienced seamen and engineers, especially in view of the demands for similar men by the armed forces. Furthermore, it is unsound for the escort vessels with a convoy to be diverted from their primary task of counter-attacking the enemy in order to rescue survivors, despite the age-old and inborn tradition of the sea which requires a ship to stand by another in distress.

By the end of 1939, after only three months of war, it was estimated that 237 merchant seamen had lost their lives as a result of enemy action, but during the following year the casualty list lengthened rapidly. By the end of 1940 the number lost had risen to 3,148, and in 1941 the grim total of 8,848 was recorded. It was not only the officers and men losing their lives who gave cause for concern, but also those who suffered permanent disability as a result of their experiences. The effect of exposure in the cold northern seas, if it did not lead to death, caused a severe form of injury known as ' immersion ' feet or hands which frequently resulted in amputation. For instance on 25th October 1941, fourteen cases of immersion foot from Reykjavik hospital, Iceland, were sent back to the United Kingdom. They were all stretcher cases, ten from the S.S. *Empire Wave* and four from the S.S. *Hatasu*, both of which had been torpedoed west of Iceland on 2nd October. The Mate of the *Empire Wave* had succeeded in navigating his lifeboat to the coast of Iceland. He started with thirty men, but two died before they were rescued by an Icelandic trawler after fifteen days at sea in an open boat with only a tarpaulin to shield them from the elements. They lived on condensed milk, chocolate, and a table-spoonful of water per man per day. The crew of the *Hatasu*, after taking to their boats, had drifted helplessly for fourteen days before they were picked up by the escorts of an eastbound convoy, into the path of which they had been driven.

Faced with a situation which clearly demanded action, the Admiralty tried the expedient of detailing the rear ships in a convoy to drop back and to endeavour to rescue the survivors of ships which had been sunk. But this proved a most unsatisfactory solution. More often than not, the rescuing ship offered herself as an even easier target to the lurking U-boat. In the case of ships sailing independently, and which fell victims to prowling aircraft or U-boats, little could be done. Survivors from these found themselves adrift on rafts or in boats, often hundreds of miles from the nearest land, or struggling in the cold waters of the Atlantic, and later the Arctic, where death quickly claimed them.

The Commander-in-Chief, Western Approaches, Admiral Sir Martin Dunbar-Nasmith, V.C., on whom responsibility for the protection of shipping in that area devolved (it included almost all the ships reaching the United Kingdom from overseas), eventually reached the conclusion that the arrangements for rescuing merchant seamen were unsatisfactory, and he stated his views in a message to the Admiralty dated 22nd September 1940 :

1. There have been several cases recently of convoy escorts following a very natural instinct and standing by torpedoed ships. At the same time it happens that the Rescue Ship detailed does not stand by the torpedoed ship.

2. If convoy escorts are to feel free to carry out their proper offensive role and the morale of the Merchant Navy is to be kept up, it is considered essential that there should be picking-up ships following astern of convoys and transferring from outward to inward convoys with the escort.

3. It is requested that the necessary ships may be taken up and sent to convoy assembly ports.

The reference to the ' Rescue Ship ' was of course to the rear ship, or to a ship in the convoy detailed to act as such, and as already mentioned this had proved a most unsatisfactory solution to the problem of rescuing survivors.

The Commander-in-Chief's message was passed for action to the Trade Division of the Admiralty Naval Staff as it was specially charged with responsibility for the movements of merchant shipping ; but the ' taking up ' of ships for Admiralty use had to be done through the Director of Sea Transport. In peace-time this was an embryo department attached to the Board of Trade ; it grew rapidly in size and importance on the outbreak of war. It acted as a go-between, the Ministry of Shipping on the one hand and the Service departments on the other, insofar as requisitioning merchant shipping for the use of the armed forces was concerned. With this went supervision of alterations to the ships to suit them for the service for which they were required. The Director of Sea Transport therefore owed an allegiance to both parties and was obliged to steer a middle course between them, a task which, as can be imagined, was not always an easy one.

Thus it was with the Ministry of Shipping and the Director of Sea Transport that the Admiralty began discussions about the type of ship required for rescue work with the convoys. Up to that time the Ministry had been very generous in meeting the Admiralty's requirements, but the heavy losses being incurred and the growing demands of shipping for military purposes had brought a realisation that we could not

afford to waste a single ton on non-essential services.
The type of ship which appeared most suitable for
rescue work was one small and handy enough to be
easily manœuvrable and with a good turn of speed,
since she must be able to overtake the convoy on
completion of her rescue operations. Ships of this
character were used in peace-time for coastwise
passenger-cargo traffic, but unfortunately not all
of them were sufficiently strongly built to stand up
to the conditions to be met with in the Atlantic in
winter. There were in fact grave doubts whether
any of these ships would prove suitable, but the need
was urgent and it was decided to make a start with a
few ships and see how they fared.

On 4th November 1940 the Admiralty was able to
inform the authorities in the United Kingdom concerned with the sailing of convoys that it was hoped
that special vessels for use as Rescue Ships would
shortly be available. Three weeks later it was announced that four ships had been taken up and that
two more would be acquired in the near future. It
had been decided after discussion with the Ministry
of Shipping that the ships should be manned by
Merchant Navy personnel, that each would carry a
naval medical officer and a sick berth attendant, and
that it would fly a Blue Ensign defaced with a gold
anchor in the fly, as worn by Fleet Auxiliaries. The
ships would be based at Greenock on the Clyde,
then the principal assembly port for ocean convoys.

The question of the status of the Rescue Ships
remained a subject for discussion between the naval
authorities concerned and the Admiralty for over a

year. In a letter to the Commander-in-Chief, Western Approaches, dated 22nd July 1942, the Flag Officer in Charge, Greenock, Rear-Admiral R. A. S. Hill, recommended their transfer to the White Ensign. He gave as his reasons simplification of procedure in dealing with them, as the Ministry of War Transport, the Director of Sea Transport and the owners would be eliminated if the ships became men-of-war. He believed that operational and administration procedure at sea would be facilitated, that discipline and efficiency would be improved, and that better supervision and training of personnel would result. But there were counter-arguments: the main one being that the Masters, Chief Engineers and crews were familiar with their ships, both as regards handling and maintenance, and that their replacement by naval personnel would mean the loss of valuable experience extending in many cases over a considerable number of years. The psychological effect of being picked up by one of their own ships also had a good effect on the morale of survivors.

The Rescue Ship organisation was perhaps a typically British compromise, compounded of complete incompatibles, which emerged as a highly efficient measure. It owed much of its success to the fact that it was composed of small-ship men, most of whom had that greatest of gifts, a sense of humour, and of men who had served together, or belonged to the same company. It was also fortunate in having as its shore organiser an extremely keen and able officer who made it his business to see that it did work. In addition to the regular deck hands and firemen, the crews occasionally included in their number a sprinkling of ' Billy ' boys from Glasgow and a few ex-convicts. Yet there never was any question about their behaviour at sea ; one and all carried out their duties magnificently, often under the most dangerous and arduous conditions. By contrast, in harbour, when tensions were relaxed, anything could happen, and on one occasion at Halifax a free fight broke out after a Christmas party, and the Mounties had to be called in to restore order.

In view of the urgent need to get the ships to sea the alterations needed to fit them for their new duties were kept to the minimum. Apart from the provision of a hospital, additional space for food and clothing and makeshift arrangements for the accommodation of survivors, little more was done to each ship in the first instance ; but gradually, as experience was gained, other improvements were made. It was difficult, however, to obtain priority for work on these ships in view of the demands being made on shipyards for the construction of new ships and the repair of those which had been damaged. Most of the vessels taken up were of the combined poop, bridge and top-gallant forecastle type, with a forward well-deck and high bulwarks and cargo doors. In some of the later vessels the forward well-decks were decked in, giving a considerable increase in the space available for survivors. In others, the top halves of the cargo doors were removed to provide suitable rescue stations forward, while the forward ends of their bridges were plated over to form watertight bulkheads. There was no previous experience to draw on to guide those charged with equipping the Rescue Ships for the object in mind—the rescue of the crews of merchant ships which had become the victims of air or submarine attack. The first requirement was clearly to provide each ship with a more serviceable lifeboat than the one it normally carried. The function of the Rescue Ship was to launch and recover her own rescue boat and also to take on board men from lifeboats and rafts, and from the water itself, in circumstances more often than not of the greatest difficulty. The rescue lifeboat was secured in mechanically-operated davits situated whenever possible at the forward end of the boat deck, so that it could be lowered alongside the straight section of the ship amidships and not get under the counter when manœuvring alongside. At first oars were used as a means of propulsion but later, when reliable engines became available, the lifeboats were power driven. If possible, two rescue lifeboats were fitted, one on each side, to avoid having to turn the ship in order to make a lee. Each voyage brought its fresh experiences and problems. The crew of a returning Rescue Ship did not talk about the lives they had saved, but of those they had failed to save. Perhaps a new set of conditions had been encountered for which the right equipment was lacking, so something was devised to fill the need and it would be tried out on the next voyage. When its usefulness had been proved, it would be adopted by the other ships. By the time the service had been in existence some two years, the Rescue Ships carried equipment to meet all known requirements.

Experience in H.M. ships had shown that a net made of rope and hung over the side was of great assistance in getting men out of the water, and they were supplied. Later, to these scrambling nets, boom nets were added. A boom net was about twelve feet wide and hung from a boom at the after end of the forward rescue station at the break of the bridge. Booms were swung out at right angles to the ship during rescue operations, and the ship proceeded at her slowest speed among the men in the water. They also proved extremely useful for stopping boats and rafts from drifting past, and held them alongside while exhausted men were taken on board. It was found that only a few survivors were capable of climbing up the nets, others being too exhausted or numbed with cold to do so. A great deal, therefore, devolved on the crews of the Rescue Ships, who were obliged to descend the nets and secure lines round the men in the water so that they could be hauled or hoisted on board. Special light davits, each with a snatch block at the head, were fitted at the rescue stations into which the lines attached to the men could be passed. When the ship rolled, the men working on the nets were often submerged, but there was never any lack of volunteers for this arduous work, in which even the firemen off watch often joined.

Small Carley floats and float-nets which could be thrown overboard, and to which men in the water could cling until they could be rescued, were also provided. Also of great value were long bamboo poles, each fitted at one end with a three-pronged

scue Ship RATHLIN

m net and Rescue motorboat

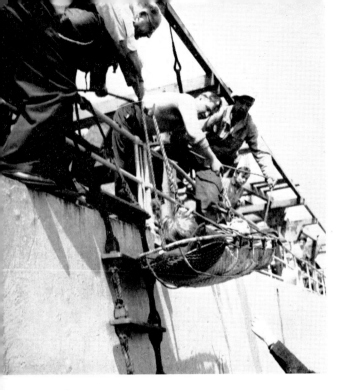

Hoisting in a stretcher

Rescue Ship EMPIRE REST

hook by which men in the water could be drawn to the side of the ship. Another useful device was a small hinged platform fitted to the bulwark aft, which, when dropped down, reached almost to the waterline. This enabled a rescuer to pick up a man who had drifted past the forward station and who was too weak to grasp any of the nets. Although each Rescue Ship was supplied with two ten-inch signalling projectors for illuminating the water when carrying out rescues at night, there was an understandable reluctance to use them unless absolutely necessary, owing to the danger of betraying her position to a lurking U-boat. There was less need to use the projectors when the red light attachment for life-jackets devised by the Ministry of War Transport came into universal use in 1942.

The choice of such small vessels for rescue work with ocean convoys may not at first sight seem ideal. When following the calling for which they had been designed, they were seldom out of sight of land for more than a few hours, and they operated mostly in waters which, even when rough, could not be compared with those to be encountered during a gale in the Atlantic. However, the ships were carefully ballasted to make them ride easily in a seaway, the best type of ballast being found to be road metal, since sand was liable to choke the bilges. To give them additional buoyancy, the free spaces in the holds were filled with empty oil drums, and the hatches secured, so that should a vessel be holed, the drums would not float away. As might be expected, the endurance of these ships was insufficient to allow

B

them to cross the Atlantic. This problem was overcome by providing additional bunker stowage, usually
by fitting a watertight door in the bulkhead between
the existing bunkers and number two hold. The
lower section of the 'tween decks could then be used
as extra bunker space. In the event, the little ships
proved themselves to be excellent sea-boats and successfully rode out some of the worst gales experienced
in the Atlantic for over thirty years, often in a better
way than ships four times their size.

The Masters of these ships, being used to close
navigation, were able to manœuvre their vessels
alongside lifeboats and rafts, and even alongside men
swimming in the water. The rescue of a boat-load
of survivors was generally a rapid evolution, whereas
the collection of men from rafts which were unable
to traverse the gap between them and the ship was
usually a longer business. To approach a single man
in the water close enough to be able to fish him
alongside with a boathook required excellent judgment. It was important to take the way off the ship
just at the right moment, so that the ship would be
stopped alongside him, otherwise there was a danger
of him being drawn into the wash of the propeller as
the engines were put astern.

Being small ships, their movement was more in
harmony with that of the lifeboats and rafts they
were assisting than would have been the case with
larger vessels. Their low freeboard too was a great
advantage when it came to fishing men out of the
water, for the most difficult part of a rescue is to get
a man up the ship's side when he is exhausted and

weighed down by sodden clothes which can increase his weight by as much as three hundred pounds.

Another factor in favour of these small ships was their speed, which in moderate weather was generally of the order of twelve knots. Even so, this gave them a margin of only two knots over the speed of a fast convoy and four knots in the case of a slow one. An excess of speed was essential, as it was obvious that when stopped to pick up survivors a ship would drop some way astern of the convoy. To be ready for any emergency, a full head of steam had to be maintained at all times, and this threw an extra load on the engineers. Had faster ships been available it would have been a great advantage ; this was most noticeable later when some sixteen-knot corvettes were taken over and converted into Rescue Ships.

So that all ships in the convoy could see that a Rescue Ship was present, the latter flew a square green flag with a white diagonal bar when first making contact. This flag was also flown when the ship was engaged on rescue operations.

An important part of the Rescue Ship organisation was the provision of emergency outfits of clothing for survivors, and toilet outfits, games and books. The Ministry of War Transport approached the British Sailors' Society, and the Society immediately undertook responsibility for meeting this need without any assurance that it would receive special funds to cover it. However, the British War Relief Society of the United States of America with great generosity came to the Society's aid and bore practically the whole of the cost of the articles supplied, a sum estimated at £22,000. A survivor's kit comprised ten articles—a jersey or cardigan, oilskin or raincoat, trousers, shoes, cap, underclothes, belt, gloves, socks and handkerchief. Also eighty libraries, each comprising thirty books, and comprehensive sets of games which included 3,072 packs of cards, were supplied.

When after a few months it became possible to send the Rescue Ships across the Atlantic to Halifax, Nova Scotia, the Canadian Red Cross supplemented the work of the British Sailors' Society by supplying additional medical equipment, especially operating tables of a type not readily obtainable in Britain. The tables were much more robust than those normally installed, and therefore better suited to the exceedingly difficult conditions with which the medical officers had to contend in rough weather. The good work of these organisations must be remembered with gratitude by all those who benefited from them. Especially notable was the hospitality extended to officers and men of the Merchant Navy by the Ajax Hospitality Organisation of Halifax, Nova Scotia.

The foregoing is a general picture of the manner in which the Rescue Service came to be formed. Starting with six practically unaltered coastwise passenger ships, it grew into a highly efficient and smooth-running organisation which was able to make a valuable and important contribution to the victory at sea. The pity was that it took the hard and cruel experience of war to emphasise the need, and cause the necessary steps to be taken to meet it.

2

The Growth of the Rescue Fleet

THE shortage of escort vessels during the first year of the war did not permit of the 'through' escort of convoys across the Atlantic. However, with the ready help of Canadian naval forces this became possible in May 1941. Meanwhile, the Admiralty gave orders that as the Rescue Ships came into service they were to be sailed with outward-bound convoys and be transferred with the escorts to inward-bound ones. In October 1940 this took place about four hundred miles to the west of Ireland.

Despite the Admiralty's desire to get Rescue Ships to sea with the convoys as soon as possible, the priority being given to anti-invasion measures and the heavy load being carried by the staff of the Director of Sea Transport, added to the formalities which have to be carried out in order to requisition a ship and prepare her for military service, caused some delay. The first ship to start operations as a Rescue Ship was the Dutch vessel *Hontestroom*. Her owners were the Hollandsche Stoomboot Maatschappij, and although she had originally been built for service to West Africa, her wartime employment was trading between London and Amsterdam. She was twenty years old and had a displacement of

1,875 gross registered tons, and she differed from
the other ships of her class in that the forward well-
deck had been covered in, giving her as it were an
extra deck forward. This detracted in some ways
from her suitability as a Rescue Ship, because
abreast the forward well-deck, as experience showed,
was the most suitable position for the rescue station
to be located, and the additional freeboard meant
that survivors had farther to climb. Also she had
only six cabins besides those used by the officers, and
most of these were required for the additional personnel needed for Rescue Ship duties. Apart from
fitting the hospital on the shelter-deck, all that was
done to equip her for her new duties was to supply
mattresses for the survivors to lie on in the 'tween-
decks. She sailed on her first voyage on 11th
January 1941.

On 24th January 1941 the Clyde Shipping Company's S.S. *Toward*, to which the minimum of alteration had been made, commenced her rescue service.
She and her sister ship the S.S. *Copeland*, which
sailed on her first trip as a Rescue Ship five days
later, were both sixteen years old when the war
began. Their maximum speed was only 11 knots,
displacement 1,526 gross registered tons. Each had
thirteen double-berth staterooms, and in that respect
they were much better than the *Hontestroom*. As
experience was gained, every time a ship returned to
port such improvements were made as could be done
in the time available; but the earlier ships never
reached the high standard of the later ones in which
it was found possible during conversion to embody

the fruits of the lessons learned with the pioneer ships.

On 28th January 1941, only four days after sailing with her first outward-bound convoy, the *Toward*, Master Captain G. K. Hudson, had the chance to prove her worth when she rescued twelve men from the crew of the British freighter *Baron Renfrew*, which had been torpedoed in very bad weather. Such a heavy sea was running that the Master was reluctant to give the order to launch the rescue life-boat; but the First Officer, Mr Knell, and a volunteer crew managed to get it away, and the survivors from the torpedoed ship owed their lives to this display of seamanlike courage and skill which was to set the pattern for the work of the Rescue Ships. On 2nd February a further twenty men were saved from the Greek ship *Olympus*, which had been torpedoed. Two days later the *Copeland* picked up eight survivors from the torpedoed anti-aircraft ship H.M.S. *Crispin*. So in less than a week forty lives were saved and the Rescue Ships had fully justified their existence. In a letter to the Director of Sea Transport, dated 24th February 1941, the Director of the Trade Division emphasised the need for yet more ships to be requisitioned for conversion to Rescue Ships. There were at the time five such ships fitted or fitting out. To the original three mentioned above, two vessels of the Pharaonic Mail Line, *Zaafaran* and *Zamalek*, had been added. These had been built in Germany and were of sound construction. Both were later to become famous in the annals of the Rescue Service.

The *Zaafaran* had been employed since the early days of the war in the general coasting trade round the United Kingdom which was maintained despite the enemy's vigorous attempts to halt it. Her conversion was begun in South Wales and completed on the Clyde. She sailed for her first voyage as a Rescue Ship on 23rd March 1941. Her sister ship the *Zamalek* had already sailed, on 26th February. Each had a displacement of 1,565 gross registered tons and a speed of 12½ knots but, although excellent sea-boats, they were not so suitable for the work required of them as the ships belonging to the Clyde Shipping Company. Neither had a recreation room for officers, apart from the dining saloon, which in itself was very small. It was found necessary to take a portion of the 'tween-decks in which to construct the hospital, and this of course reduced the amount of space available for survivors. The cabins too were on the small side; but eventually, by the display of much ingenuity, it was found possible to provide accommodation in each ship for twenty-six officers in cabins and fifty-six survivors in berths in the 'tween-decks. On deck, space was at just as great a premium as it was below, as the ship's lifeboats and the rescue motorboat occupied nearly all the available room. When it came to fitting a winch for rescue work, there was nowhere to put it except over the engine-room skylight.

The *Zamalek*'s Master, Captain Owen C. Morris, D.S.O., had commanded his ship in peacetime on trading voyages between Alexandria, ports in the Levant and the Black Sea, and he handled her with

the skill of a born seaman. His award of the D.S.O.,
one of the very few given to officers of the Merchant
Navy, was earned during service with the Arctic
convoys. An account of this is given in Chapter 4.
On his second voyage in *Zamalek* as a Rescue Ship,
Captain Morris was faced with a rescue operation of
a particularly hazardous nature. The British ship
Benvorlich, carrying a large quantity of ammunition
and explosives, was torpedoed and caught fire.
Captain Morris, fully aware of the nature of the
cargo she was carrying, proceeded at full speed towards her in an endeavour to take off her crew before
it was too late, but while he was still some distance
off the *Benvorlich* blew up with a deafening roar,
raining large pieces of jagged metal over the area.
Captain Morris was narrowly missed by a piece of
boiler plating weighing several pounds which fell on
the bridge beside him. Arriving on the scene of the
disaster, the *Zamalek* was able to rescue the twenty-
four surviving members of the *Benvorlich*'s crew,
including her Master, who recovered from his
wounds but was thereafter only fit for shore service ;
four of the other survivors died later in hospital.

On 28th February a vessel belonging to the Dundee,
Perth and London Shipping Company, S.S. *Perth*,
was requisitioned for the Rescue Fleet. She was
larger than any ship so far allocated, having a displacement of 2,589 gross registered tons and a speed
of 13 knots. She was a veteran of the First World
War, having been completed in 1915 and then
immediately requisitioned for service as an Armed
Merchant Cruiser. She saw plenty of action during

B 2

operations against the Turks in the Red Sea, having
taken part in the bombardment of Jedda in June
1916, when 1,200 German and Turkish prisoners
were captured. She crowned her war service by
sinking an enemy submarine on 1st October 1918.
After that eventful start to her career she was returned to her owners, and for the next twenty years
she was employed on the company's service between
Dundee and London. In October 1940, because of
her considerable passenger accommodation, she was
used as accommodation ship for the workmen employed in completing the new battleship H.M.S.
King George V, which had been moved from the
Tyne to Rosyth, where it was considered she was
less vulnerable to enemy air attack.

The *Perth* was different from all other Rescue
Ships in that she had no holds which could be fitted
with bunks for survivors. The forward holds were
used as reserve bunkers, and the space amidships
was taken up by passenger cabins on two decks. It
was decided therefore not to alter this arrangement ;
but although she was one of the largest of the Rescue
Ships she could only accommodate just under a
hundred survivors in single and double berth cabins.
It was not realised when this decision was made that
survivors suffering from shock would react against
being shut up in cabins and would prefer the company of their fellow survivors in the more open spaces
in the ship, where there was also easy access to the
upper deck in the event of further trouble. This
being so, after a large number of survivors had been
rescued they tended to crowd the upper deck

and to interfere with the work of the crew when carrying out further rescues. The hospital was also rather sub-standard. The smoking room used for this purpose was small and there was no separate room for an operating theatre; so the operating table was sited in a corner of the hospital. When an operation was in progress the other patients had a full view of the proceedings, and this did not add to their peace of mind.

At about the same time another railway vessel, S.S. *Melrose Abbey*, was selected for conversion. Built in 1929, she had a displacement of 1,908 gross registered tons, a speed of 13½ knots, and appeared to be an excellent choice. Unfortunately, on her way round to the Clyde to be converted she ran ashore at Newburgh Minch on 31st March 1941, and despite repeated efforts she was not refloated until 26th July. In fact, it was very doubtful at one time whether she would ever be salved, as she was driven farther up the beach by the unfavourable weather which set in after the first attempt to refloat her had failed. Then a mine drifted alongside her and exploded, blowing a hole in her side; this added to the difficulties of salvage. However, she was eventually refloated and towed to Aberdeen for temporary repairs, and thence to the Clyde. These mishaps delayed her conversion, and she was not ready to sail on her first voyage until 12th May 1942.

The months of March, April and May 1941 witnessed a great increase in the number of merchant ships lost as a result of air attack, and on 3rd May 1941, on her first voyage, the *Perth* was called upon to rescue the crew of the frozen-meat ship S.S. *Somerset*, which had been hit in the after well-deck by a bomb dropped by a lone enemy aircraft which dived on her out of the clouds. The *Perth* immediately closed her and, when it was seen that she was sinking, took off the entire crew numbering sixty, some of whom had minor injuries.

On 30th May 1941 a meeting, over which the Director of the Trade Division presided, was held at the Admiralty. It was attended by representatives of the Ministry of War Transport, and the administration of the Rescue Ships and the need to provide more of them was considered. The Flag Officer in Charge, Greenock, had put forward to the Admiralty, in a letter dated 15th May 1941, a number of suggestions for adding to the efficiency and improving the general running of these ships as a result of experience gained to date. These covered the supply of better rescue boats, additional radio operators, loudhailer equipment for communicating with damaged ships and with men in the water, improved accommodation for rescued personnel, and many other matters. While all the items were important, one which was to have considerable influence on the success of the Rescue Ship organisation was the realisation that the arduous work performed by the ships and the particular nature of their service earned for them special consideration on their return to harbour—upriver berths, if possible alongside, where repairs could be expeditiously carried out, improvements made, and the crews given a chance to get ashore. Responsibilities were inevitably divided between the Principal Sea Transport Officer in the Clyde and the owners or agents of the ships working in co-operation with the Ministry of War Transport. It was evident that the appointment of an officer to co-ordinate all these requirements would be most advantageous, and in June 1941 Lieutenant-Commander L. F. Martyn, R.N.V.R., of the Principal Sea Transport Officer's staff at Greenock, was given this important task, and he discharged it almost unaided from then on until the end of the war.

The Rescue Ships were armed, since they made no claim to being hospital ships under the Geneva Convention, and they were painted grey without any distinguishing marks. As we have seen, they were subject to attack like any other ship at sea, so it was decided to make use of their presence in convoys by fitting them with special high-frequency radio direction-finding sets (HF/DF). This would enable them to locate enemy submarines in the vicinity which were in the habit of using this form of radio for communicating with each other. As the apparatus was not yet in general use in H.M. ships, the Rescue Ships were able to play an increasingly important part in the battle against the German U-boats, a battle which was soon to work up to its climax and become one of the bitterest struggles fought out at sea. Additional accommodation had to be provided for the naval personnel required to man the guns and for the extra radio operators required to keep continuous watch on the HF/DF sets. A further requirement was extra stewards and cooks to cater for the survivors. Each ship's crew was also increased by nine men to allow for manning the rescue motorboat and assisting with the rescue work.

As a result of the Admiralty meeting, the Director of Sea Transport redoubled his efforts to find further vessels suitable for conversion to Rescue Ships. It had been decided that, because of her unsuitability, the *Hontestroom* should be withdrawn from the Rescue Service and returned to trade, and that her place should be taken by the Union Castle Mail Steamship Company's S.S. *Walmer Castle*. She was a little ship of only 906 gross registered tons, but she was diesel-driven and capable of a speed of 15 knots. She was the first ship to have a thorough conversion, and her hospital and operating theatre were better than anything yet provided in other ships. Because of her small size, her hatches were decked over with steel plates : it was expected that she would ship a lot of water in a seaway. She sailed on her first voyage in her new role on 12th September 1941, in company with the escort of the Gibraltar-bound convoy OG74. On 19th September she rescued twenty-three survivors from the S.S. *City of Waterford*, a victim of air attack. The following evening two ships of the convoy, *Empire Moat* and *Baltallin*, were torpedoed, and with some difficulty the *Walmer Castle* rescued the entire crew of thirty from the former and twenty-eight survivors from the latter. These operations took some time, and touch was lost with the convoy. But before sailing, each Rescue Ship was provided with a series of positions through which the convoy would pass, so as to enable her to rejoin it if separated. Just before noon on the following day, while *Walmer Castle* was still endeavouring to overtake the convoy, she was attacked by an enemy aircraft which dived out of the sun. The Master, Captain G. L. Clarke, took up a position on the bridge outside the wheelhouse, from which he could watch the enemy's movements. The aircraft flew down the fore and aft line of the ship and released a bomb, but the Master put the helm hard over at just the right moment and the bomb fell in the sea. A second attack was made, followed by a third, and regardless of the incendiaries and the hail of machine-gun bullets with which the enemy sprayed the ship on each occasion, he stood on the open bridge watching the aircraft approach and skilfully dodging each bomb. Meanwhile the ship's gunners were making a determined reply to the enemy's attacks every time he came within range, while the rest of the ship's company dealt with the incendiaries, several being killed or wounded while doing so. During the third attack Captain Clarke was hit in the stomach by a bullet, but he insisted on remaining at his post on the bridge. The enemy returned for a fourth attack, and this time a bomb struck the bridge close to where the Master was standing, killing him instantly. It tore through the hospital, penetrated two decks and exploded on top of the engine-room, wrecking all the machinery below, including the pumps supplying the fire main. A fire which was impossible to control broke out, and the ship was soon a blazing inferno amidships. A human chain was formed to rescue the injured survivors trapped in the hospital. The end man would dash into the smoke, grab a man and drag him to the chain, which would then bring him to safety. The rescued men were then placed in the starboard lifeboat, the only one remaining intact. This got away with forty-two. Others were placed on two rafts which had to be hurriedly cast off, as by this time the side plating amidships was red hot. Thirteen of the crew remained on board, including two severely wounded men and one old man. They gathered on the poop to get away from the intense heat of the fire, and while they were there the magazine blew up. Had it not been for the timely arrival of the corvettes H.M.S. *Deptford* and *Marigold* to rescue them, they might have shared the fate of the eleven officers and twenty men who had lost their lives during the attack, and but for the magnificent efforts of the ship's officers and crew, the overall casualties would have been much heavier. Captain Clarke was posthumously awarded the Lloyd's Medal and Commendation. So was Cook H. V. Hill, who gallantly shielded a shipmate from the aircraft's machine-guns at the cost of his own life. Also decorated for bravery were the Chief Officer, A. Lawson, the First Radio Officer, W. T. McGowan, the Boatswain, A. C. Davies, and Steward J. Piccirillo. The most satisfactory feature of this gallant encounter was the destruction of the attacking aircraft. It was shot down by an aircraft of Coastal Command patrolling round the convoy, the pilot reporting afterwards that the enemy's tail had been severely damaged by the *Walmer Castle*'s gunfire.

The loss of this Rescue Ship added urgency to the

need to increase the numbers. In July four more ships had been taken up for conversion. These were the Clyde Shipping Company's vessel S.S. *Rathlin*, the London North Eastern Railway Company's vessels S.S. *Dewsbury* and *Stockport* (both over thirty years old, which is a good age for any ship, however carefully maintained), and the Danish ship S.S. *Tjaldur*, which had been seized in the Faeroe Isles on 16th June 1941 and released by the Prize Court for service under the Crown. All were ready for service during October, but the *Tjaldur* soon proved that she was too small and too unseaworthy, and had to be withdrawn after only three months' service.

On her first voyage the *Dewsbury*, under her gallant Master Captain A. J. E. Snowden, O.B.E., saved two survivors from the British ship *Kirnwood*. The men were clinging to an upturned lifeboat. The *Kirnwood* was one of three ships torpedoed in an outward-bound transatlantic convoy, and altogether fifty-five survivors from them were picked up, nearly all by the escort vessels and trawlers with the convoy.

The function of a Rescue Ship and the facilities which it was able to supply were not at first properly understood, but later, when these had been sufficiently promulgated, the competition between the escort vessels and the Rescue Ships to pick up survivors ceased, and the latter were left to get on with the job for which they had been provided while the escort vessels properly concentrated on sinking the U-boats.

On 15th August 1941 another old 'railway' ship, S.S. *Bury*, was taken up, but on her passage from the Tyne, where she had been converted, round to the Clyde, it was found that the wooden deck which had been built over the after well-deck was insufficiently strong to stand up to winter gales in the Atlantic, and it had to be replaced by a steel one. This delayed her entry into service until 27th December. A similar alteration had to be made in the *Dewsbury*. But although everything was done to make these ships as comfortable as possible, their great age and the weight of the defensive armament which they had to carry encouraged the development of leaks which were hard to check.

Even with these additions, which brought the number of Rescue Ships up to nine, there were not nearly enough to enable one ship to be sailed with each convoy. Moreover, the convoy commitments were increasing. In July 1941 the transatlantic convoys were split into fast and slow sections in order to make better use of ships capable of speeds in excess of 10 knots. There were now regular convoys running between Britain and Gibraltar and Britain and Freetown. Thus there were always at least a dozen convoys at sea on any one day, sometimes as many as fifteen. Then in 1942 a further, and what was to prove most exacting, commitment arose with the introduction of the Arctic convoys between Britain and North Russia. The part played by the Rescue Ships in these is one of the most stirring in the history of the Second World War. It was estimated that to provide for all these convoys, thirty Rescue Ships would be needed. So there was still a long way to go.

3

De Profundis

On 3rd December 1941, as evidence of the success of the Rescue Ship organisation, the Principal Sea Transport Officer for the West of Scotland was able to inform the Admiralty that so far 616 lives had been saved by the Rescue Ships and that they had also brought back to the United Kingdom 444 survivors who after rescue had been landed in Iceland. Since its occupation in May 1940, Iceland had proved of increasing value as a halfway station for the air and sea forces supporting the transatlantic convoys. As such, it was also a convenient port for the escort vessels and trawlers to land men picked up from ships sunk in mid-Atlantic, but they then had to be brought back to Britain. Since in the early days the Rescue Ships did not cross the Atlantic, it became customary for them to call at Reykjavik to pick up survivors before joining a homeward-bound convoy. It was not a very satisfactory arrangement as it meant that the space which should have been reserved for further casualties was often taken up by passengers. For example, on one occasion in the summer of 1941 the Rescue Ship *Zamalek* embarked one hundred and six members of the crews of two ships which had been sunk, and these took up all her available accommodation, including some of the ship's officers' cabins. Fortunately she was not called upon to rescue others on the way home.

In February 1942 the Director of Sea Transport informed the Trade Division of the Admiralty that six of the nine additional vessels which had been asked for had been provided. These were the *Dewsbury, Rathlin, Stockport, Bury, Gothland* and *Accrington*, and all except the last were already in service. However, he went on to point out that the balance of ships needed could only be met by allocating cargo vessels, and he indicated that the Ministry of War Transport would resist any further demands made on them for Rescue Ships. As has been mentioned, the choice of vessels suitable for rescue work was limited and, highly important as the Service was, the Ministry had to take other factors into consideration. When quite early in the war the East Coast ports became unusable for deep-sea ships, a very heavy strain was thrown on internal transport, and in this vessels of the Coasting and Short Sea trade played an essential part. At one time these ships were carrying a volume of goods greater than that of the entire overseas import programme. Outlying islands like the Orkneys, Shetlands and Faeroes had to be kept supplied, and although ideally the solution would have been to construct new ships specially designed for the job, the pressure on the shipyards for repairs and for new ships to replace those sunk ruled this out. The Ministry of War Transport had no option therefore but to accept the situation, albeit with great reluctance.

Also in February 1942 history was made when the *Copeland* achieved the first crossing of the Atlantic by a Rescue Ship and berthed at Halifax, Nova Scotia. Her arrival created much interest in the Canadian port, and led to the establishment of a link with the Canadian Red Cross, the benefit of which was to prove extremely valuable. There had been much doubt about the ability of these small and ancient coasting vessels to stand up to the violence of Atlantic winter gales but, thanks to fine displays of seamanship by their Masters, they weathered some of the worst storms ever known in that part of the world, although not without damage. In January 1942 the *Dewsbury*, Master Captain A. J. E. Snowden, O.B.E., escorting an outward-bound convoy, ran into very heavy weather when four days out. She lost one of her lifeboats and had two others severely damaged, and the bridge ladders were carried away. The two-inch-thick teak doors leading to the midships accommodation were smashed to pieces by the force of the waves, giving the sea access to nearly a third of the quarters below decks. By good seamanship and quick work on the part of her crew, and with the help of tarpaulins and spare hatch covers, the watertight integrity of the ship was restored, but it was a foretaste of what was to be expected and of what many of the other Rescue Ships also had to endure. The Admiralty agreed to Rescue Ships proceeding right through with the convoys bound for Gibraltar, and on this run too the weather was often almost as great a hazard as the enemy.

In the early part of 1942, although the focus of the struggle in the Atlantic shifted to the eastern seaboard of the United States, U-boats were also operating in mid-Atlantic. On 22nd February the Rescue Ship *Toward*, Master Captain A. J. Knell, was escorting a convoy which was attacked when six days out from the Clyde. The British ship S.S. *Adellon* was hit in the engine-room and sank within a few minutes. The *Toward*'s rescue boat, still only a pulling one, was launched, but after two hours searching it had rescued only six survivors. However, five more were picked up by the ship herself by means of lines thrown to them. The following day the S.S. *Inverader* was hit, but the Rescue Ship managed to save the entire crew of forty-two before she went down. While rejoining the convoy, Captain Knell noted that the Norwegian motor vessel *Eedanger* had also become a casualty and was sinking, so he closed her and took off thirty-nine members of her crew. An anxious moment occurred soon afterwards when a surfaced U-boat was sighted. It dived immediately ; fortunately no attack developed.

As a result of the experience gained during this voyage, two important additions were made to the equipment of the Rescue Ships. These were the boom nets, described in Chapter 1, and motor rescue boats to replace those of the pulling type. In consequence the efficiency with which the Rescue Ships were able to carry out their duties was greatly improved.

In March 1942 a record figure of 834,164 gross registered tons of Allied shipping was sunk, sixty-four per cent of it in the North Atlantic, and the demand for Rescue Ships by the authorities responsible for operating the convoys grew accordingly. Typical of the splendid work being performed by the few ships available is the story of the thirty-two-year-old Rescue Ship *Bury*, Master Captain L. E. Brown, O.B.E., which sailed on her fourth voyage with Convoy ON592 on 5th May 1942. During the first few days of the voyage H.F. direction-finding bearings taken by her radio operators indicated that submarines were closing in on the convoy, and Captain Brown was eventually able to tell the senior officer of the escort and the Commodore of the convoy the time and direction from which an attack might be expected. His estimate proved correct. On the night of 12th May the British ship S.S. *Llanover* was torpedoed. Hearing the explosion, the *Bury* at once proceeded to the scene and succeeded in rescuing forty-five survivors of her crew in as many minutes. Later, rejoining the convoy, she came across twenty-one survivors of the torpedoed S.S. *Empire Dell*, all of whom were rescued in less than an hour. After searching the area for further survivors, the *Bury* proceeded at her best speed to overtake the convoy, which the Master had observed was then under heavy attack. While doing so he came across the wreck of the *Llanover*, the Master of which asked to be put back on board with a volunteer crew. However, it was evident that she was sinking so the attempt was not made. Next, thirty-eight survivors of another victim of U-boat attack, S.S. *Cocle*, were rescued. One man was so badly injured that he died soon afterwards. On re-joining the convoy the *Bury* was ordered to search another area, and three hours later she sighted three boats containing thirty-four survivors from the Swedish ship *Tolken*, which had sunk after being hit by two torpedoes. A little farther to the northward she came across two more lifeboats, and from them forty survivors of the torpedoed British ship S.S. *Batna* were picked up. With 178 survivors on board in addition to his own crew of sixty-two, and with food running short, Captain Brown was given per-mission to make for the harbour of St John's, New-foundland, which he reached safely.

It is not surprising that when reports such as these reached the Admiralty, representations were again made to the Ministry of War Transport for the pro-vision of further Rescue Ships as a matter of urgency. It was also suggested that inquiry be made in the United States for suitable vessels, but unfortunately this source was to prove unproductive.

Meanwhile, all through the summer of 1942, as the Battle of the Atlantic worked up to its desperate climax, the nine available Rescue Ships continued their good work. On her third voyage, the *Gothland*, which had been the first Rescue Ship to reach Gib-raltar, was escorting an outward-bound transatlantic convoy on which U-boats were known to be closing. In the early hours of 12th June the British ship *Dartford* was torpedoed and sunk, and although she did not get off a distress signal, and the night was more than usually dark, the *Gothland* made over in the direction from which the noise of the explosion had come, and soon found herself in the midst of wreckage. Four men were sighted clinging to an up-turned lifeboat and four more were seen on a raft. All these were quickly rescued by the ship's hand-propelled lifeboat which the Master, Captain J. M. Haddon, O.B.E., decided was preferable to the motor lifeboat on account of the amount of wreckage strewn over the area. Seven more men clinging to pieces of wood were also taken on board, the difficulty of their rescue being increased by the fact that most of them did not have the red flashing lights which were subsequently a standard fitment on life-jackets. Two of them were even without jackets. The last man to be picked up was the *Dartford*'s Chief Engineer, but the time he had spent in the water proved too much for him and he died as a result of exposure.

On 24th August the Rescue Ship *Stockport*, Master Captain T. E. Fea, O.B.E., on her sixth voyage, while attached to the slow outward-bound trans-atlantic Convoy ONSC122, was called upon to rescue the crew of the British ship *Sheaf Mount*, which had been torpedoed. The motorboat was lowered, and while she was away the ship herself trawled up forty survivors from the Latvian S.S. *Katvaldis*, which had shared a similar fate. Mean-while, the motorboat had collected twenty-six of the fifty-seven members of the *Sheaf Mount*'s crew, but although an extended search was made the remainder were never found. While engaged on this operation, the *Stockport* received a signal indicating that another ship had been torpedoed, but thick fog prevented her from finding the new casualty, the survivors from which were picked up by one of the escorts. But now HF/DF bearings indicated that there were a number of U-boats between the *Stockport* and the convoy. Captain Fea doubled the lookouts and ordered his gun's crews to maintain utmost vigilance. The fog grew thicker and visibility dropped to a few yards. Just after he had managed to contact one of the convoy escorts and establish his own identity, Captain Fea distinctly heard the sound of a U-boat surfacing, although he could not see anything. The enemy was out of luck, for he was spotted by the escort vessel, which was able to engage the submarine at close range and sink her. Captain Fea saw the gun flashes and heard the sound of firing but he never saw the U-boat. The Rescue Ships were indeed in the thick of the battle.

In his report the Master stated that the behaviour of the whole crew was excellent, and that the work was done smoothly and with speed. The arrangements for the medical care of the survivors was also in every way satisfactory. The boom nets had proved of great value, and all the survivors from the *Katvaldis* were picked up by this means. The senior officer of the escort, in H.M.S. *Viscount*, signalled to Captain Fea : ' Everyone is filled with admiration at the way in which you carried out your rescue duties, knowing as you must have done that there were more U-boats in the vicinity than thought possible. Allow me to congratulate you on your invaluable aid to the convoy.'

Returning to the United Kingdom on the homeward leg of her fourth voyage, the *Gothland* ran into

very heavy weather when seven days out of Halifax.
The convoy was in the dangerous area which at that
time could not be covered by shore-based aircraft
from Canada, Iceland or Britain, when at the height
of the gale, at three a.m. on 13th October, the enemy
submarines delivered a concerted and sustained
attack. Several ships were torpedoed within a short
space of time, one of them being the whale factory
ship S.S. *Southern Empress*, which went up in flames
and lit up the sea and the convoy for miles around.
Captain Haddon described the weird sight thus
created—the white combers of the breaking waves,
the red distress rockets soaring into the air from the
stricken ships, the brilliant light of the snowflake
rockets fired by the escort vessels searching for the
surfaced enemy ships, and the thunder of exploding
depth charges. Men could be heard crying and
screaming for help among the wreckage, but as they
had no lights they could not be seen, and the heavy
sea and swell made it impossible to lower a boat.
Every effort was made to save them, but without
success, and it was with a deep feeling of remorse
that Captain Haddon left the area to go to the rescue
of two more ships which had been torpedoed. He
manœuvred his ship carefully among the men in the
water and in boats and on rafts, and by this means
was able to ' trawl ' them into his ship's side, where
the willing hands of his crew hauled them to safety,
often at the risk of their own lives. In this manner
twenty men were rescued from the Yugoslav motor
ship *Nikolins Matkovic*, and a further twenty-one
from the Philippino ship *Susana*. Making a wide

sweep round the area of the attack, the *Gothland* successfully rescued thirty-nine men from the British S.S. *Empire Mersey*. The still-burning wreck of the *Southern Empress*, belching a huge column of black smoke, was then investigated for further survivors, but none was found. After spending twenty-four hours searching the area, Captain Haddon set course to rejoin the convoy.

The gale had been followed by fog, and two days later the convoy was again attacked. The *Gothland*, which by now had resumed her station in the convoy, hearing the sound of gunfire, steered towards it. While the lookouts were peering through the fog, watching for damaged ships, they suddenly sighted the dim grey silhouette of a submarine. Captain Haddon put his helm over and attempted to ram, but the U-boat disappeared from view, and although the senior officer of the escort was informed of the sighting by radio telephony, the enemy presumably took refuge beneath the surface, as she was not seen again.

Many of the eighty survivors now on board the *Gothland* were in a very bad way as a result of exposure and wounds, and the ship's Medical Officer and his staff, aided by members of the ship's company, worked night and day to provide medical treatment and comfort for these men. The rescued officers and men from the sunken ships who were fit doubled the lookouts and helped in every other way possible. Both Captain Haddon and his Chief Engineer D. McAddie were awarded the O.B.E. for their splendid rescue work during this voyage.

The gale which buffeted the *Gothland*'s convoy was in fact the tailend of a West Indian hurricane which, following the usual path of such phenomena, had recurved to the north-east on reaching more temperate latitudes. While the *Gothland* escaped the worst of it, the Rescue Ship *Bury* escorting an outward-bound transatlantic convoy encountered its full fury. The first sign of its approach was a rapid fall in the barometric pressure which began about noon on 17th October. This was accompanied by a freshening of the wind which by nine p.m. had reached full gale strength, causing a confused and dangerous sea, and obliging the ships in the convoy to heave to. A great gust of wind ripped off the canvas lookout position on top of the *Bury*'s bridge, and as the ship pitched and rolled ever more violently Captain Brown, at his position in the wheelhouse, peering through the driven spray dimly saw a mountainous wave rear itself up on his port side, to crash down inboard seconds later with a thunderous roar. The little ship was thrown over almost on her beam ends, and when she slowly righted herself he found that the engine-room and stokehold were flooded, the radio aerials had carried away, the port bulwark was flattened against the fore-deck, and the rafts on the port side and their steel supports had collapsed and stove in the hatch to Number Two hold, into which tons of water had poured. There was damage too to bridges, rigging and boats.

Fortunately the head of steam was not lost, though the fireman in the stokehold had been seriously injured when he was flung against the bulkhead as the ship heeled over. The pumps were immediately started in an endeavour to rid the ship of the tons of water which she had shipped. While the Master was wondering whether his little vessel would survive the violence of the storm, and all hands were striving to repair the damaged hatch cover, he sighted the bright glare of snowflake rockets on his port beam, indicating that enemy submarines were attacking the convoy, and this, as he well knew, meant casualties. A few minutes later he received a message informing him that a tanker, the U.S.S. *Angelina*, had been torpedoed. An agonising choice now faced him. Should he attempt a rescue with his ship in such a parlous state, or should he follow the dictates of prudence and consider the safety of his own ship first ? To a man of his stature and experience, only one answer was possible. He turned his battered ship in the direction of the stricken tanker, although this brought her beam on to the sea and the risk of once again being engulfed by another great wave, an event which would almost certainly have spelt her doom.

The forty-three members of the *Angelina*'s crew abandoned ship in one lifeboat. They had just managed to pull clear of the stricken vessel when the boat broached to as a mighty comber bore down upon it. Its vicious white crest towered above the unfortunate men, then it crashed down, capsizing the boat and throwing them into the water. When it had passed, only half their number remained struggling to get a hold on the upturned hull. The waves tossed and battered them as they clung to the bilge rails on the bottom of the boat. The water was cold, and after a while hands and feet went numb; finally one by one they slipped away, too tired to continue the fight for life. But there was one of their number, the ship's carpenter, Gustav Alm, who would not give up, and he continued to exhort his shipmates to ' Hold on ' until help arrived. Time and again when a man was swept from his hold, Alm went after him and brought him back. But despite his efforts the numbers dwindled. When the *Bury*, steaming at her best speed of four knots, reached the scene six hours later, only four men besides the carpenter remained.

The Master of the *Angelina*, Captain W. S. Goodman, and a few others had climbed on to rafts and they were sighted by the *Bury* before she reached the lifeboat. Four men were rescued with considerable difficulty, the crew of the *Bury* having to go down the scrambling nets and haul them aboard. One moment they were high in the air, the next in water up to their necks, as the little ship rolled and pitched in the mountainous seas. Unfortunately Captain Goodman was lost when the painter of the raft to which he was clinging broke and he drifted away. Although the rescue motorboat was launched in an effort to save him, it was quickly swamped, and the boat's crew had a narrow escape from drowning.

Some time later the capsized lifeboat was sighted, and with great skill Captain Brown manœuvred his ship until she was within a few feet of it. He had to take care not to get so near as to risk injury to the men on the boat should it be dashed against his ship's side ; it required the nicety of judgment which only an experienced seaman could provide. A heaving line was thrown, and the brave Alm half raised himself in an effort to grab it. Twice he missed it, but at the third attempt he managed to grasp it and make it fast through one of the hand-grips in the bilge-rails. His four companions were too far gone to be able to assist him. Four more lines were thrown from the *Bury*, and Alm made one fast round each of the men, and then freed the men one by one so that they could be hauled on board. But by the time a line was thrown for him he was almost at the end of his tether. Summoning up the last ounce of his strength, he managed to make it fast round his waist, and when he was hauled up on to the *Bury*'s deck he was bruised, bleeding and covered with oil. He was given a tot of whisky and fell fast asleep.

For his heroic conduct Gustav Alm was awarded the Distinguished Service Medal of the Merchant Marine by the United States Maritime Administration, and after a few weeks' rest he went back to sea. Writing to the Maritime Commission, Captain Brown said that he felt honoured to have been able to play a part in the rescue of such a brave man, a man America could be proud of.

The *Bury* reached the port of Halifax, where repairs were made to the damage she had suffered in the gale. On her return voyage she added to her growing reputation by securing first-class bearings of enemy submarines converging for an attack on

Transferring men in a basket

Artificial respiration

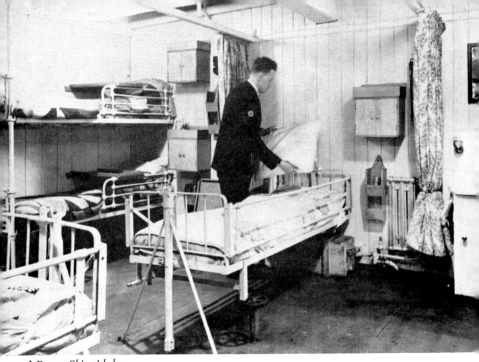

A Rescue Ship sick-bay

Rescue Ship operating theatre

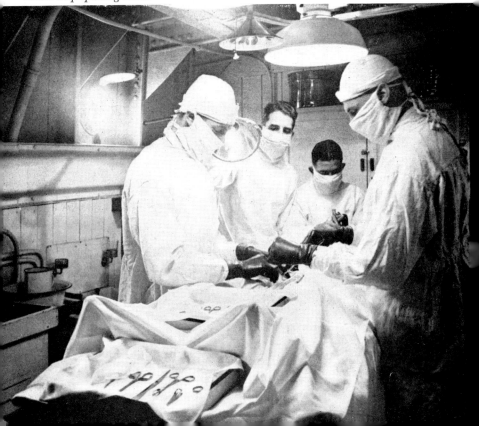

the convoy to which she was attached, and by sub-sequently successfully rescuing members of the crew of the U.S.S. *Brilliant*, which caught fire after being struck by a torpedo but which was subsequently brought into port.

We must now return to the Rescue Ship *Stockport*, escorting the homeward-bound convoy SC107 which left Halifax on 27th October 1942 and was sighted by a U-boat patrol off Newfoundland three days later. HF/DF bearings obtained by the *Stockport* clearly indicated that the U-boats were closing to make a massed attack; but before they were able to do so they lost two of their number to air-craft of the Royal Canadian Air Force. On 1st November, when the convoy passed beyond the range of air escort from Newfoundland, there were still seven U-boats in contact with it. At five minutes past midnight the attack began, and it con-tinued almost incessantly for the next thirty-six hours. To the Master of the *Stockport* it seemed as if a succession of ships were being torpedoed and a never-ending stream of survivors was being picked up. The first ship to be hit was the *Empire Sunrise*; her entire complement of fifty was saved. Three hours later the British ship *Dalcroy* was torpedoed, and again the whole crew, numbering forty-nine, was picked up. Almost at the same time the Greek steamer *Rinos* was hit and, while proceeding to the rescue of her crew, the *Stockport* almost collided with the wreck, which was floating bottom up. Twenty-six survivors were rescued out of a crew of thirty-one. During this operation the *Stockport's*

C

Chief Officer, Mr H. K. Earnshaw, made use of a holed and water-logged lifeboat from the sunken ship to collect men from a raft, and in the boat they sat in water up to the thwarts. On return to the ship, Mr Earnshaw was so exhausted that he could not climb the scrambling net. He fell back into the sea, but was quickly rescued.

Next the British ships *Empire Antelope* and *Empire Leopard* were torpedoed simultaneously. The whole crew of the first ship was saved, but the second ship blew up and there were only four survivors, one of whom subsequently died.

On 3rd November, when the *Stockport* was re-joining the convoy she was badly shaken by a violent underwater explosion. As a result, the main deck was set up on the starboard side, and the boat and upper decks, the forepeak and number one hold developed leaks. At first it was thought that the ship had been torpedoed, and some of the survivors on board rushed the boats and cast them adrift. Drastic action was taken to restore order. Several ships in the convoy also felt the explosion, and some false alarm signals were made. It was afterwards believed that an enemy submarine had blown up under the convoy, but post-war records do not show any recorded loss of a U-boat on that date.

Meanwhile the weather began to deteriorate, and by five o'clock the following evening it was blowing hard. The *Stockport* was preparing to rescue the survivors of another victim of the attack, the American ship *Parthenon*, and was going astern to take the way off the ship when her propeller struck an abandoned steel lifeboat. This brought the engines up with a round turn. Although most of the boat fell clear, some part of it remained fast, and for the next eight hours every revolution of the propeller was accompanied by a loud thump on the stern frame. Because of this the ship's speed was reduced to $8\frac{1}{2}$ knots; but despite the mishap twenty-three out of the twenty-nine members of the *Parthenon*'s crew were rescued.

The loss of speed left the *Stockport* with very little margin over that of the convoy, and while she was still some way astern, endeavouring to catch up, another American ship the *Hahoia* was torpedoed. All but three of the crew of fifty-six were rescued. Because of the number of U-boats about, Captain Fea was reluctant to stop and lower his motor rescue boat, but by skilfully manœuvring his ship, and with the aid of the boom nets, down which members of his crew went to help men out of the water, the rescue was made without difficulty.

The whole thirty-six-hour rescue operation is an unsurpassed achievement in the annals of the Rescue Service. A total of two hundred and fifty-six officers and men were saved in difficult and dangerous circumstances, thanks to the skill and devotion to duty of the officers and men of the *Stockport*. In his report the Master stated that from the time the first sinking took place just after midnight on 1st November until his ship reached Iceland six days later, he and his officers were on their feet practically the whole time, without rest. For this splendid achievement Captain Fea was awarded the O.B.E., but alas, by the time it was gazetted, he and his gallant ship had been lost with all hands on another rescue operation. On 24th February 1943, while on escort duty in mid-Atlantic, in response to a distress signal from a ship straggling astern of the convoy, the *Stockport*, which already had ninety-one survivors on board, turned back. She was never heard of again.

By no means every voyage made by the Rescue Ships had endings either as dramatic or as tragic as those which have just been described. The *Perth*, under her first Master Captain Keith Williamson, O.B.E., made fifteen voyages, during which she was called upon to carry out only four rescues. But the risk of a major disaster was ever present, and one night in the winter of 1942 she found her resources taxed to the uttermost.

At eight p.m. on 17th November the outward-bound convoy to which the *Perth* was attached was set upon by a pack of U-boats, and two ships were torpedoed almost simultaneously. The Rescue Ship stood by the Greek ship *Mount Taurus*, which sank very quickly, and picked up thirty-eight of her crew from rafts, boats and out of the water. She then searched the area for survivors from the other ship, but none was found, and after five hours she rejoined the convoy. At three a.m. on the 18th the U-boats struck again. This time they torpedoed and sank the American ship *Parismina*, and the French ship *President Sergeant*—in which the Commodore of the convoy was embarked. Fifty-four members of the American ship, all numbed with cold, were rescued with great difficulty. The *Perth*'s crew had to go down the scrambling nets and make lines fast to the men in the water so that they could be hoisted out. By the time they had finished, they were almost as cold and wet as the men they had rescued. Some of the crew of the *President Sergeant* had left their ship in lifeboats, although it was still afloat. They had drifted away, so the *Perth* had to go in search of them. When the occupants of these boats had been rescued, she returned to the wreck and took off the ten men remaining on board. Amongst those saved were the Commodore, J. N. Brook, R.N.R., and the Master, Captain P. Dove, who was making his first trip since his release from the German prison ship *Altmark* by Captain Vian (now Admiral of the Fleet Sir Philip Vian) in H.M.S. *Cossack*. A Chinaman from the *President Sergeant* had dived from the ship's bridge and had landed head first in the bottom of one of the lifeboats. He was suffering from a compound and depressed fracture of the skull, a broken wrist, and complete left-sided paralysis. In the *Perth* Surgeon Lieutenant Kelly, R.N.V.R., decided that an operation to remove the piece of bone pressing on the brain was necessary immediately if the man's life were to be saved, and he asked the Master to nurse the ship as much as possible while this delicate surgery was performed. As the two sick berth attendants were busy looking after the survivors, an off-duty radio officer volunteered to act as anaesthetist. The ship was steaming slowly along on a course which would keep her as steady as possible. A critical point in the operation had been reached when there was a shout from one of the lookouts on the bridge : " Submarines approaching from the starboard quarter." Captain Williamson went on to full speed and opened fire with his twelve-pounder gun, at the same time taking violent evasive action to put the enemy off his aim. These tactics proved successful and the *Perth* got away. Despite these extremely adverse circumstances the surgeon carried on with the operation. It proved successful, and the Chinaman was subsequently landed at Halifax with every chance of a complete recovery.

Meanwhile the *Perth*, which by then had on board one hundred and thirty-six survivors, had fallen a long way astern of the convoy, and the Master knew that enemy submarines were following in its wake, and so between him and his allotted station. Later that afternoon he sighted some U-boats on his port bow, but the corvette H.M.S. *Rose*, which had dropped back to harry them, managed to keep them from interfering with the *Perth* as she regained her station. Although further attacks on the convoy were threatened none actually developed, and the Rescue Ship reached Halifax safely with her company of survivors.

During her homeward voyage, the *Perth* was required, at midnight on 7th December, to rescue the crew of a tanker loaded with aviation spirit which had been torpedoed and had caught fire. The tanker was fitted with Admiralty Net Defence but it had been streamed only on one side, and the crew were just about to put out the nets on the other side when she was struck forward in number one tank. She was soon a blazing inferno from stem to stern, and as Captain Williamson approached her it did not seem possible to him that there could be anyone left alive on board. However, he continued to close her, and found to his astonishment the whole of her crew in the water clinging to the Net Defence on the windward side. It was a ticklish business rescuing them, but in the end fifty-seven were hauled on board. Very soon afterwards another ship, the *Charles L. D.*, was torpedoed, turned turtle and sank almost immediately. Ten men were trawled up from the sea and a further two were rescued from rafts; all were suffering from cold and exposure, although they had been in the sea for only a short time. The Master of the sunken ship said he had no recollection of being saved, having lost consciousness.

So the work of the Rescue Ships went on in the Atlantic, but their services were in even greater demand in another and yet more dangerous area.

4

Arctic Odyssey

ON 28th May 1942 the Admiralty informed the Senior British Naval Officer, North Russia, that four oil-burning Rescue Ships had been allocated for service with the convoys which, since September of the previous year, had been running more or less regularly between Britain and North Russia. This meant depleting the already inadequate number of Rescue Ships available for the North Atlantic convoys but, as experience was to show, the need for these ships with the Arctic convoys was even greater.

For the first few months, enemy opposition to the convoys carrying much needed military equipment and supplies to Russia had been surprisingly weak, and by the end of 1941 fifty-three ships had made the voyage without loss. In the New Year, however, there were signs that resistance to this traffic was to be stepped up. In March 1942 the powerful battle-ship *Tirpitz* had been sailed to intercept a convoy of sixteen ships bound for Murmansk, and but for bad weather and a lack of air reconnaissance she might well have found and destroyed them. With the coming of the summer, better flying weather, and continuous daylight throughout the twenty-four hours, the chances of interception were greatly increased, and the enemy therefore decided to strengthen his air, surface and submarine forces in the area in an effort to halt the running of the convoys. In May intelligence reports indicated that a large number of aircraft had been moved to airfields in North Norway, from which they could cover the last half of the convoys' route. Ships bound for Murmansk had no option but to run the gauntlet of air opposition, since the port itself was within a few minutes' flying time of the enemy airfields at Petsamo and Kirkenes. Even ships bound for Archangel five hundred miles to the east could not avoid coming within range of attack, because of the ice barrier to the north. Since the route of these convoys was restricted by geographical and physical factors, the task of the enemy U-boats deployed to intercept them was made easier. And the enemy believed that neither his submarines nor his surface ships in the area to the east of the North Cape, known as the Barents Sea, were likely to encounter any opposition from British carriers and heavy ships, which had not so far penetrated it. Russian opposition both in the air and on the surface was discounted. In the summer of 1942, therefore, the dice were heavily loaded against the merchant ships sailing in the Arctic convoys.

It was to a convoy known as PQ17, a designation to become world famous, that the first Rescue Ships were allocated. They were the *Rathlin* (Captain A. Banning, D.S.O.), *Zaafaran* (Captain C. K. McGowan, D.S.C.), and *Zamalek* (Captain Owen C. Morris, D.S.O.), and the inclusion of three such ships

c 2

in one convoy was evidence of the Admiralty's concern for the safety of the personnel of the thirty-five merchant ships which it was intended should sail in it.

These three Masters were outstanding members of their profession. Captain Banning, born at Lockerbie, Dumfriesshire, was a Lowlander, and being of medium build and only five feet four inches in height was known to his friends as ' Wee Banning '. Besides being a fine seaman, he was an authority on the life and the works of Robert Burns. He had been for many years with the Clyde Shipping Company, and had gained his Extra Master's Certificate. He was in command of the company's ship *Beachy* when she was bombed and sunk on 11th January 1941. He was rescued by a trawler, and could only be given first-aid for a broken leg, so he suffered thereafter from a limp. But this did not interfere with the performance of his duties. He has been described by one of his officers as ' one of the finest seamen I was privileged to sail with '. A stickler for duty, he took an immense pride in his work, his ship and his crew. By contrast, Captain McGowan was a big man with the faraway look acquired by men with long experience of the sea. Captain Morris was a Welshman with an intimate knowledge of the Levant, where his ship had been trading for most of her life. He was a man of medium build but he had the heart of a lion. In port his powerful tenor voice could be heard echoing from his cabin in a series of operatic arias, with which he was well-acquainted.

The *Rathlin* and the *Zamalek* sailed in company from the Clyde on 23rd June 1942, joined the anti-aircraft ships *Palomares* and *Pozarica* and four corvettes, and proceeded in company with them to Seydisfiord on the east coast of Iceland. Here they found the *Zaafaran*, which had left Loch Ewe with the British section of the convoy and reached the anchorage two days previously.

The convoy, half of which flew the United States flag, assembled at Hvalfiord, an inlet close to Reykjavik on the west side of the island. From there it sailed on 27th June, routed along the west and north coast of Iceland and thence to Archangel, Murmansk having been temporarily put out of action by bombing. (The Russian Commander - in - Chief, Northern Fleet, Admiral Arseni Golovko, in an entry in his diary for 2nd July, comments : ' Now that Murmansk has in effect ceased to exist as a town, we have just received a hundred A.A. guns for its defence! ')

One ship ran aground on leaving the anchorage, and another suffered damage from ice and had to return. So when the Rescue Ships and the rest of the escort joined the convoy to the north of Iceland on 30th June it comprised only thirty-three ships and a naval tanker for refuelling the escorts. The escorts included six destroyers, three minesweepers and four anti-submarine trawlers ; also a squadron of four cruisers which, however, had orders not to proceed beyond the longitude of the North Cape. All on board this valiant armada were tense and expectant, having been warned that their passage was likely to be stoutly resisted by the enemy.

On 1st July a German reconnaissance aircraft

located the convoy to the north-east of Jan Mayen
Island, and from then onwards it was continuously
shadowed, the U-boats taking over when the aircraft lost touch.   The air temperature was 34°F according to Surgeon Lieutenant R. D. Wilkins,
R.N.V.R., the Medical Officer of the *Rathlin*, whose
official report provides a valuable factual account of
the epoch-making voyage.   (Wilkins was a power-
fully-built man with side whiskers and a beard which
gave him a remarkable resemblance to King Henry
VIII as portrayed by Charles Laughton.)   The following day he recorded, ' Still very cold. . . .   The
morale is still good in the ship but the tension is
growing, more marked by lack of sleep and the
knowledge that the most dangerous part of the
voyage is yet to be encountered.'

   That day the first attack on the convoy by torpedo
aircraft took place.   The *Zamalek* was carrying as
deck cargo a large launch with an R.A.F. blue, white
and red roundel clearly marked on the after canopy.
Unfortunately this appeared to have a particular
attraction for the German pilots, and every time an
attack took place *Zamalek* was singled out for special
attention.   On this occasion three of her A.A. gunners were wounded when the ship was sprayed with
machine-gun bullets ; but they had their revenge
two and a half hours later when they shot the floats
off a seaplane which attempted to repeat the process.
It crashed near by.

   Throughout the next day enemy aircraft circled
the convoy and carried out sporadic but unsuccessful
attacks.   Several icebergs were seen, but otherwise

the day proved uneventful. The 4th July began in-
auspiciously when, at 1.50 a.m., in bright daylight,
a lone Heinkel torpedo-bomber dived out of the
clouds and torpedoed the United States ship *Christopher Newport*. The *Zamalek* was quickly on the
scene and rescued forty-seven members of her crew
of fifty; three men had been killed in the engine-
room when the torpedoes hit. The sea at the time
was as smooth as glass, with cloud level at between
three and four hundred feet, a factor which favoured
the enemy aircraft in making a surprise attack. All
day long aircraft circled the convoy, keeping the
defenders on the alert, as if attempting to wear down
their resistance. In the evening they struck. Dr
Wilkins was standing on the deck of the *Rathlin* at
the time. ' At about 1800 hours the circling German
planes were suddenly joined by between thirty and
forty Heinkel torpedo bombers which approached at
tremendous speed a few feet above the sea on the
starboard quarter. All our guns went into action
and a terrific barrage was put up by the convoy,
which forced the aircraft to turn to port, but did not
prevent them from firing their torpedoes into the
heart of the convoy. The leader pressed home the
attack in a very daring manner, passing straight down
the lines of the convoy and being shot down in
flames. Two torpedoes passed ahead of us, one
actually under our bows, and three astern.' Despite
the determined way in which the attack was delivered,
only three ships were hit. These were the British
Navarino, the American *William Hooper*, and the
Russian tanker *Azerbaijan*. Eight men from the

Azerbaijan either jumped or were blown overboard, and one had a broken leg. They were rescued by the *Zaafaran*, Captain McGowan collecting them in one smooth, beautifully-planned swoop. The *Zaafaran* picked up thirty survivors from the *Navarino*, while the *Rathlin* recovered forty-four from the *William Hooper* and nineteen from the *Navarino*. Eleven more of the *William Hooper*'s crew were rescued by the *Zamalek*. Despite the expeditious manner in which the rescues were made, there were several cases of shock and hysteria. One negro who had been blown off the after gun-platform of his ship and had spent between fifteen and twenty minutes in the ice-cold water was severely shocked, but after treatment he slowly recovered. Each survivor was issued with a full set of clothing, given a tot of rum, food and cigarettes, and allotted a bunk. But it proved ' very difficult to keep men from staying on deck . . . and at every alarm there was a mad stampeding of humanity on to the upper deck.'

It was late that evening, just as the three Rescue Ships were rejoining the convoy on completion of their work, when a signal was received from the Admiralty ordering the convoy to scatter and the cruisers to withdraw to the westward, where they were to be joined by the destroyers. It is outside the scope of this book to discuss the reasons which led to the taking of this momentous decision. Suffice it to say that it was not made without the most careful consideration of all the factors involved, chief of which was the presence in the area of the German battleship *Tirpitz*.

It may be that the order was given prematurely, but now that we know the facts it seems clear that, whatever action had been taken, the convoy was bound to suffer severe losses. The receipt of the order came as a terrible shock to the morale of the crews of the merchantmen, and especially to those in the Rescue Ships loaded with survivors. They saw the cruisers and destroyer section of their escort disappearing at high speed over the western horizon without being aware of the reasons which had prompted such drastic action.

In the Merchant Navy, the Royal Navy is often referred to as ' The Grey Funnel Line ', and when the message was received in the *Zaafaran*, Captain McGowan sent for Surgeon Lieutenant MacBain, R.N.V.R., greeting him as he stepped on the bridge with " Look what your shipping firm's done now! " A conference ensued, in which the Mate took part, to decide in what way the order to ' Scatter ' applied to the Rescue Ships. They reached the conclusion that while the order implied that each ship should fend for herself and not risk being sunk by standing by another ship, this did not apply to them. As the Mate put it, " We are only under orders when we are in convoy ; now we are on our own, we abide by the usual custom of the sea and give help wherever we can."

In accordance with the instructions laid down for such an emergency, the *Rathlin* headed north towards the ice-barrier at her best speed. The *Zaafaran* and *Zamalek*, together with an Admiralty tanker, the *Aldersdale*, steered north-eastward. The

ships of the convoy followed the divergent courses
laid down for them, before resuming the course
which would take them to Archangel. So PQ17,
which on the evening of 4th July had been a coherent
body of ships steaming eastward in orderly array,
became thirty independent vessels engaged in what
was to prove a hopeless and costly *sauve qui peut*.

The *Rathlin* reached the ice-barrier on 5th July,
turned eastward, and fell in later that day with the
anti-aircraft ship *Pozarica* and one of the corvettes
of the former convoy escort. The sound of gunfire
and bursting bombs echoed over the southern horizon, but luckily visibility along the ice-edge was poor
and the ships were not sighted by the enemy aircraft
which, together with a number of U-boats, were now
scouring the area in search of easy victims. The
Pozarica and the corvette eventually drew ahead of
the *Rathlin*, but before parting company the former
informed *Rathlin* that she was making for the coast
of Novaya Zemlya. On 6th July the *Rathlin* encountered the United States freighter *Bellingham*, and the
two proceeded in company. ' We had to alter course
many times to avoid running into ice,' recorded Dr
Wilkins. After making the coast of Novaya Zemlya
and altering to the southward, the *Bellingham* signalled that she had a case of suspected appendicitis.
The *Rathlin* hove to with a fair sea running, and
lowered the motorboat to take Dr Wilkins on board.
Although it was not an acute case, he decided to
bring the man back with him for observation. In
the event, he made a quick recovery.

The following day the two ships encountered large

formations of ice barring their path to the southward, and they were obliged to turn and steam north-west in search of open water, a course which inevitably brought them back into the danger area. All day long distress signals from ships and from boats' radio sets were intercepted, many from vessels sunk several hundred miles from the nearest land. It was not long before the *Rathlin* and her big consort were sighted by a patrolling Focke-Wulf Condor, and it attempted to bomb them. ' The pilot must have felt sure he could deal with us himself' wrote Captain Banning. ' I was glad he didn't call out the dive bombers, for they were only some twenty minutes' flight away. He flew into the attack himself. The *Rathlin* opened fire, well and truly aimed, setting the plane on fire and it crashed into the water, a blazing mass.' When the ship closed the wreckage to pick up survivors, she found that all six members of the crew were dead.

The explosion of the bombs had broken some ammonia bottles in the *Bellingham* and she was obliged to stop for half an hour to rid the engine-room of the fumes. Later the two ships proceeded, and the following day they made a landfall at Syvatoi Noss on the Murmansk Coast, whence they were escorted by a Russian gunboat through the Gourlo and into the White Sea. They reached Archangel safely on 9th July.

The *Zaafaran, Zamalek* and *Aldersdale* were not so fortunate. By the morning of 5th July the three had become separated, the *Zaafaran* having drawn ahead, although she was still in sight on the horizon. There was a long-standing rivalry between the Chief Engineers of the Rescue Ships, going back to the pleasanter times of peace ; and now that they were no longer in convoy, Miller in the *Zaafaran* was anxious to show his opposite number Dawson in the *Zamalek* which was the faster ship. The visibility that day was extreme, and from the *Zamalek*'s bridge five other ships of the former convoy could be seen on various bearings. Two of these, the minesweeper *Salamander* and the freighter *Ocean Freedom,* joined forces with the *Zamalek* and the tanker, and the five vessels proceeded in company. But a few hours later they were subjected to an attack by four dive-bombers and the *Aldersdale* was hit. The *Salamander* quickly rescued the crew while the *Zamalek* beat off the attackers, a reversal of roles which in the special circumstances was undoubtedly justified, since the Rescue Ship carried the more formidable A.A. armament of the two, besides already having fifty-eight survivors on board.

Meanwhile the *Zaafaran,* some nine miles to the eastward and quite alone, was attacked by a JU88 dive-bomber. From a height of five thousand feet the aircraft swooped on the little ship. At three thousand feet it released a stick of bombs, and although Captain McGowan put his helm over in an effort to dodge them, the middle bomb of the stick struck his ship on the starboard side abreast the engine-room. The engines stopped immediately and the ship listed to starboard. When Chief Engineer Miller reported that the engine-room was filling rapidly and that the flooding could not be controlled, the Master ordered the ship to be abandoned. He said in his report that had it not been for the buoyancy drums stowed in the lower holds she would have gone down like a stone, as the explosion had practically cut her in half, and that besides the engine-room, number two hold was also open to the sea. Only the rescue motorboat and one lifeboat were intact. These were lowered and filled with the survivors, the crew taking to the rafts. The ship's Medical Officer, Dr Mac-Bain, and the Mate, M. G. Longfield, were among the last to leave the sinking ship and together they went over the side. The temperature of the water was 32°F. ' I was fifteen minutes in the water before being able to get on board a raft which floated up from the wreck,' wrote Dr MacBain in his report of the incident. ' On boarding the raft, skin anaesthesia was complete to the neck. Joint sense was impaired and there was a well-marked ischæmia (white, dead fingers) of both hands and feet. Massage and work at an oar restored sensation rapidly and painlessly, except in the fingers where sensation returned slowly, still showing traces after eight weeks.' He attributed the fact that those who like himself were obliged to jump into the freezing water did not succumb because they went in fully clothed.

All the while the *Zaafaran* had been drawing ahead of the *Zamalek* there had been an exchange of rude and witty signals between the two ships. All eyes on the *Zamalek*'s bridge were therefore focused on their faster rival. When it was seen that she had been hit, Captain Morris called on his Chief Engineer to ' give her all he'd got ' and raced towards the stricken ship, reaching her after some fifty minutes of hard steaming. The anti-aircraft ship *Palomares* had also seen the attack, and she closed in and provided protection to the *Zamalek* while she was picking up survivors. A total of ninety-seven were rescued, and these included the thirty-eight survivors whom the *Zaafaran* had previously rescued. Only one man was lost. " Now," said Chief Engineer Dawson to Chief Engineer Miller as the latter climbed over the side, " which is the better ship ? "

The *Zamalek* had on board one hundred and fifty-five survivors in addition to her own crew, so she was particularly vulnerable to attack. Dr MacBain at once placed himself at the disposal of his colleague in the *Zamalek*, Dr McCallum, and although, fortunately, there were no cases of serious injury on board, the two Medical Officers were fully engaged coping with cases of hysteria and shock which, had they not been promptly dealt with, might have led to panic. ' Generally morale among survivors was undoubtedly low,' recorded Dr MacBain. ' This appeared to be due not so much to lack of personal courage, as to a combination of several factors.' He set these out at some length, and because they explain so clearly the basic problems with which the Rescue Ships' Medical Officers had to deal, they are worth recalling :

1. In action the survivors have nothing to do.
2. Both officers and men have recently been manning ships, not as passengers, but as part of the ship's company. In consequence everyone from Master to Fireman criticises the work of his opposite number in the Rescue Ship. The latter must, therefore, leave no loophole for adverse criticism or loss of confidence,

especially as the survivors are usually ' deep sea ' men while the
crews of the Rescue Ships are not.

3. Survivors for a varying period after being picked up are
very ' lifeboat ' and ' raft ' conscious. As I know from personal
experience and discussion with others, the alarm bell automatically
brought visions of impending disaster, and caused one to rehearse
mentally the action of abandoning ship. Therefore, to remain
below was difficult.

4. In a crowded ship it is obvious that there is not enough
lifeboat or raft accommodation for everyone.

5. There is a tendency for men to assume that since they are
passengers their officers no longer have any authority over them.
The fact that the officers know this saps their confidence and
deprives one of the advantage which their leadership and example
would provide.

6. In contrast to the above, the way in which the D.E.M.S.*
gunners picked up, quickly became part of the naval organisation
within the Rescue Ship, was most marked.

But the *Zamalek*'s troubles were not yet over. She
followed the *Palomares* to an anchorage in Matochkin
Strait, which separates the two halves of Novaya
Zemlya. There she was joined by a group comprised
of five merchant ships, three minesweepers, three
trawlers and the corvette *Lotus*. The *Lotus* had
gallantly turned back to rescue survivors from the
Commodore's ship, the *River Afton*, which had been
torpedoed and sunk by a U-boat. She picked up
Commodore J. C. K. Dowding, R.N.R., who was
found floating on a raft.

A conference called by the Captain of the *Palomares* was attended by the Commodore, Captains and
Masters of all the ships present. It was decided that
no time must be lost in vacating the exposed position
in which the ships were anchored. The boat taking

* Defensively Equipped Merchant Service

the Masters of the merchant ships back stopped first
at the *Zamalek*, and Captain Morris invited them on
board for a drink.   It is a tribute to his outstanding
personality that what had been a party of tired and
dispirited men left his ship in an almost ' devil may
care ' frame of mind which was not entirely due to
alcohol.   Jokingly they renamed Matochkin Strait
' Funk Creek ', and suggested that a medal should be
given to all those there.   It was to have a yellow
ribbon embroidered with white heather!

Commodore Dowding resumed charge of the re-
mains of his once proud convoy, and as soon as all
ships were under way and ready to proceed he led
them south towards Archangel.   They sailed on the
evening of 7th July and immediately ran into fog.
This persisted until midnight on 8th July.   On that
day one of the merchant ships lost touch and returned
to the anchorage.   Every now and then boatloads of
survivors from ships which had been sunk were encountered, and the occupants were taken on board
the minesweepers and trawlers, since it was impossible for the *Zamalek* to take any more.   As the ships
proceeded south, an increasing number of ice floes
were met, and at one time the *Zamalek* stuck fast in
the ice and had to go astern to get clear.   At eight a.m.
on 9th July the Commodore decided that it would
be wise to seek more open water to the west, even
though this meant increasing the risk of being de-
tected and attacked by a still watchful enemy.   Sure
enough, that evening, when they were only about
sixty miles off the Russian coast, air attacks commenced, and continued without a break for several

hours. On board the *Zamalek*, taking passage to North Russia, were Commander Humphrys Archdale, D.S.C., R.N. and an Air Staff Officer who had placed themselves at Captain Morris's disposal. Morris stationed them one on each wing of the bridge, while he himself stood by the wheelhouse ready to give instant orders to the helmsman. All three worked as a team. An eye-witness recalls hearing the two officers on the wings calmly exchanging remarks like " Yours I think " as they gazed skywards watching the fall of the deadly missiles and estimating their trajectories, punctuated by Captain Morris's crisp commands " Hard a-port " or " Hard a-starboard ". Once again the *Zamalek* appeared to be the centre of attraction for the enemy bombers. But so skilfully was she manœuvred that she managed to avoid being hit. There were plenty of near misses, some very near indeed, unshipping the standard compass and drenching all those on the bridge with spray. Finally a near miss bursting abreast the engine-room fractured the main oil supply pipe, and the engines had to be stopped ; it also broke the dynamo bedplate and put out the lights. Although in complete darkness except for the light of a torch, Chief Engineer Dawson, assisted by his former rival the cheerful and portly Chief of the *Zaafaran*, Miller, and by the Chief Engineer of the American ship *Christopher Newport*, managed to repair the damage and the ship was able to get under way again.

All the while the ship's gunners were busy beating off attack after attack, Commodore Dowding watched the action through binoculars. He stated after-

wards that he frequently thought the *Zamalek* had
gone when she disappeared from sight amidst clouds
of spray thrown up by the bomb splashes. But each
time the gallant little ship emerged like an angry
terrier, barking defiance at her enemies.

It is not surprising that the strain of this continuous
attack told on some of the survivors on board the
Zamalek. When the ship was stopped these men tried
to launch a boat and leave her. Fortunately they
were restrained from doing so. But Captain Morris
was to describe his own ship's company as ' grand '
—one of the understatements of all time. He particularly praised his gunners who, because of the
continuous daylight, could never leave their guns,
but who were ready at all times to beat off an attack.
Their efficiency was undoubtedly instrumental in
saving the ship.

When the attacks finally ceased, a moving incident
took place. The A.A. ship *Pozarika*, Captain E. D. W.
Lawford, R.N., closed the *Zamalek* and for a
moment all on board the Rescue Ship thought there
was going to be a collision. Then they noticed that
she had manned ship and, steaming close past, the
Pozarika's company cheered *Zamalek* to the echo.
' As the caps went up and the sound floated across,
all of us felt unexpectedly moved,' wrote Dr Mac-
Bain. Captain Lawford, standing on the wing of his
bridge, called to Captain Morris on the loud hailer :
" I would greatly appreciate your ensign if you have
done with it." Glancing aft to the tattered remnants
of the Blue Ensign streaming from the peak halliards
like a battle flag in a picture of a sea-fight of old,

Captain Morris shook his head. In a few well chosen words he thanked the *Pozarika* for the protection given to his ship but concluded, " Even so, you're not getting that ensign—its MINE."

At four o'clock on the afternoon of 11th July the *Zamalek* berthed safely at Archangel, but because of the lack of accommodation ashore only half of her one hundred and fifty-four survivors could be landed, the remainder continuing to live on board. Although they did not know it at the time, their stay in North Russia was to be a long one.

It was not until 24th July, after Commodore Dowding had returned from a further search of the Novaya Zemlyan coast bringing in six more ships, that it was possible definitely to assess the losses suffered by Convoy PQ17. They amounted to twenty-three merchant ships sunk, and the Rescue Ship *Zaafaran*, and were the most severe suffered by any mercantile convoy during the war.

5

Russian Interlude

WHILE Commodore Dowding was away searching for
further survivors from the ships of his devastated
convoy, information was received by the Senior
British Naval Officer, Archangel, Captain Guy
Maunde, D.S.O., R.N., that there were one badly-
wounded man and ten survivors suffering from
severe cases of immersion feet at a small Russian
settlement in the bleak and desolate area of Novaya
Zemlya. A Russian doctor was in attendance but he
admitted to being unable to cope with the situation.
At that time, the title of ' Doctor ' in Russia could be
assumed by anyone who had done two years in a
medical school. A fully-qualified medical practitioner
earned the title of ' Professor ', a fact which may
account for the unfortunate predicament of the
doctor in question.

Captain Maunde asked Dr Wilkins of the *Rathlin*
to fly up to the settlement in a Russian aircraft which
was about to leave on one of its routine visits to
meteorological stations in the Northern Command.
Dr Wilkins was accompanied by the United States
Naval Attaché, Commander Franckel, U.S.N., who
was anxious to see what could be done to salvage a
large American freighter, the *Winston Salem*, which

had run aground in Moller Bay on the west coast of Novaya Zemlya, 650 miles north-north-east of Archangel, whilst escaping from the German air and submarine onslaught.

They left Archangel on 19th July, and reached the air base to find that the flying boat in which they were to travel, an American-built Catalina, was already loaded with ten Russian passengers, six crew and a large quantity of stores for delivery to stations *en route*. (The pilot had the distinction of being the first Russian to fly across the North Pole and land in America.) Dr Wilkins had brought with him medical stores and equipment for emergency surgery, cigarettes, tea, sugar and blankets, and with the addition of these the aircraft was so overloaded that, despite three attempts, it could not take off. The pilot decided that he would have to off-load some of the fuel. This done, the aircraft took off and flew through the night to the Kara Sea. There a landing was made near the first station on the schedule. The party went ashore for a meal, and took off again two hours later. The next stop was made at a lake on the mainland, where the flying boat was refuelled and another meal was taken. " I do not know what the food was," said Dr Wilkins, " but it consisted of some form of meat floating in fat." Each man was provided with a fork with which he was expected to spear morsels from the communal platter. Soup, black bread and vodka completed the repast. Three hours after landing they were again airborne, with five hundred miles to go to the next station at Moller Bay, on the coast of Novaya Zemlya. When they arrived it was shrouded in dense fog, so they returned to the lake from which they had taken off. They waited twelve hours for a favourable weather report, and on the following attempt they were able to alight at their destination, having had a narrow escape from an encounter with a German reconnaissance aircraft. Here Commander Franckel left the aircraft to attend to the salvage of the *Winston Salem*, the crew of which had left their ship and were encamped ashore.

When the time came to take off again the sea was too rough, so a Russian trawler towed the flying boat some ten miles up the coast to another more sheltered bay. There it was able to get into the air. After an hour's flight they reached the station where the injured men were reported to be. After landing, Dr Wilkins was greatly disappointed to find that his long and difficult journey was wasted. The casualties had been embarked in a surviving ship from the convoy, the British *Empire Tide*, which had called at the anchorage only a few hours previously. The flying-boat pilot relieved him of most of his stores and equipment, assuring him that they would be used to replace those expended at the station by the ' doctor '. But Dr Wilkins considered that the chances of the food and cigarettes ever leaving the aircraft were poor. He gave the pilot some instruction in first-aid treatment for immersion foot, in case he should come across any cases during the rest of his flight, and stressed the importance of not using heat, as the ignorant might be expected to do. Then he embarked in a Russian trawler.

The trawler steamed south, and after a voyage

lasting twenty-four hours it reached the position where the *Winston Salem* was aground. Dr Wilkins went on board. Meanwhile, Commander Franckel had persuaded the crew to return to the ship, and after two attempts, and with the aid of two Russian tugs which had arrived, she was refloated. Escorted by three Russian trawlers she shaped course for Archangel, and although she was twice sighted by German aircraft fog came to her rescue and she was not attacked. This was just as well, because the crew had thrown the breech blocks of her guns overboard when they abandoned the ship. After a voyage lasting seven days the ship berthed at Molotovsk, one of the subsidiary ports of Archangel.

When Dr Wilkins arrived back at Archangel he found that the doctor appointed as Base Medical Officer had not arrived and that Captain Maunde had requested Dr MacBain to take up the post. Dr MacBain had made great progress in getting things organised. He had been ably assisted by the Chief Radio Officer of the *Zaafaran*, Mr C. Wolf, who, unlike a great many of the survivors, was anxious to make himself useful. Dr MacBain set up a Sick Bay in a loft above some stables and, while he and his faithful sick-berth attendant Bryant were away trying to contact the sick and wounded survivors, Wolf got busy. By the evening, when they returned, he had furnished the place with furniture improvised from packing cases, had begged, borrowed or stolen some chairs and a typewriter, and had started to make out a nominal list of survivors. From then on he became unofficial Medical Administrator, keeping records of the cases dealt with and relieving the Medical Officers of the other paper work with which they would otherwise have had to cope themselves.

In view of the constant threat of air attack, Dr MacBain arranged for the dispersal of the medical stores. This wise precaution was to pay off.

A Corporal of the R.A.M.C. had been installed in the Intourist Hotel to attend to the numerous cases of illness among the survivors billeted there, and arrangements had been made for definite hours of attendance by a Medical Officer at the other buildings where survivors were housed, as well as for consulting hours at the Naval Base.

In addition to the one hundred and fifty-five survivors in the *Zamalek* and the sixty-three in the *Rathlin*, the *Empire Tide* and the other ships brought in by Commodore Dowding had collected a further two hundred and forty. These, with the survivors picked up by the corvettes, trawlers and minesweepers brought the total to almost 1,300. They presented to the Russian authorities a problem with which they were ill-equipped to deal. Not only was there a great shortage of food and clothing amongst their own people, but the only accommodation available to house such a large number of survivors was most primitive. An eye-witness account of the scene which greeted the British and American seamen when they stepped ashore is provided by a Rescue Ship's officer :

One of the mates and I went ashore to have a look round the town. The enclosed yard seemed to be full of junk of all sorts including a large collection of church bells and miscellaneous scrap metal. Outside the yard there was a pathetic open market laid out by the roadside, consisting of broken dishes and crockery, bottles, rag dolls, door locks and handles, etc. We proceeded along the main street on the raised and broken sidewalk, past boarded up shops and burned out buildings. A heavily escorted working party of prisoners passed by. A queue of muffled up women stood outside a closed baker's shop. A small group of mourners shuffled along preceded by a coffin on a two-wheeled handcart—and silence, a silence you could feel. Nobody spoke. A silence broken only by the loudspeakers suspended at the street intersections, blaring out at intervals what we took to be pep talks—long harangues and martial music. We returned to the ship infinitely depressed, almost ashamed of our smart uniforms amid so much squalor.

In contrast to the cold experienced during the voyage, the weather at Archangel was very warm and mosquitoes abounded. ' The anti-mosquito ointment provided has no deterrent effect, in fact it appears to encourage their appetite,' recorded Dr Wilkins.

Among the survivors there were a number of medical cases suffering from frostbite, immersion foot and other injuries. Captain Goodwin, R.A.M.C., the resident British Medical Officer, was confronted with the difficult task of arranging hospital accommodation for the casualties. Although the Russians willingly lent ambulances, they were unable to produce them at short notice. Matters were complicated by a shortage of interpreters, and any attempt to get things moving was invariably met by *zafterer*, the Russian equivalent of *mañana*, so that what should have been an hour's job often took a day to accomplish.

At first both sick and fit survivors were accommodated in the Sevroles Hospital, but as the numbers grew a large school was taken over and the fit were transferred to it. This was a three-storey building, having numerous large rooms which were converted into dormitories. The Russians did their best to provide reasonable comfort, but their standard was very much lower than that to which the British and American seamen had been accustomed. The beds were hard and there was much bed-bug infestation. In spite of drastic action taken to deal with the pests, they were never entirely eliminated. Sanitation arrangements were appalling owing to the lack of water pressure.

Messing also presented difficulty. At first men were taken in batches to the Sevroles Hospital for meals, but as numbers increased the shortage of transport put a stop to this ; so the authorities took over a near-by restaurant. The food consisted mainly of black bread, soup and a kind of buckwheat porridge which, if unpalatable, was at least nourishing. For all its monotony, the diet was better than that available to the civilian population. Most marked was the shortage of green vegetables.

It was not long before the survivors discovered the local ' black market ', in which a bar of chocolate or a packet of cigarettes fetched fifty to a hundred roubles (one to two pounds sterling), to be promptly exchanged for illicit vodka, usually of the most inferior quality which, in some cases, contained wood alcohol. The drinking of this was the cause of much illness and two recorded deaths. One of the after-effects of indulgence was an extreme thirst which

Typical crew members of the Rescue Ships

Chief Radio Officer Horace Bell of the COPELAND
and ZAMALEK

Captain O. C. Morris, D.S.O., and the Officers and Crew of Rescue Ship ZAMALEK

Captain L. E. Brown, O.B.E.

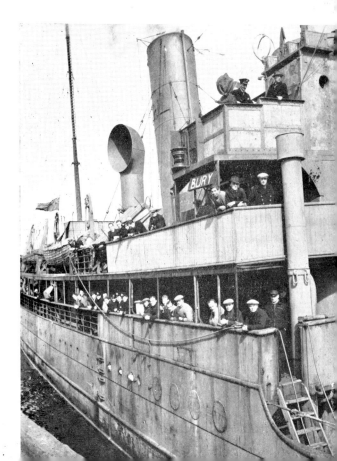

Rescue Ship BURY arriving
Halifax with survivors

S.S. Angelina, United States of America Torpedoed October 17th, 1942 at 2345 in the North Atlantic.

To the Captain, Officers and Crew of the SS Bury:
On the night of October 17th, 1942, although battered and crushed by a raging gale, you turned your sturdy little ship into the sea to rescue us, the few survivors of the SS Angelina, torpedoed and lost through enemy action. Words cannot express our gratitude but we can never forget the gallant ship Bury and her brave men who courageously perform a mission of rescue on the war-torn seas. Men of a great nation which will always be victorious.

Harry E. Brown, Ensign, USNR   E. Koenig Chief Officer
Van D. Turner S. 2. C. U.S.N.R.   M. Salvide - Murman
Charles J Barrell S 2/c U.S.N.R.   Gus Alm Carpenter
Eli Coffee S 2/c U.S.N.R.   Diego Martinez Steward

The survivors of s.s. ANGELINA. *The splendid Gustav Alm is in front, wearing a cap*

caused men to drink water from the nearest tap instead of waiting to obtain a boiled supply. As the water was pumped from the Dvina, into which the town drains were emptied, it is not surprising that the results of drinking it were often disastrous.

Although games and athletics were organised, and cinema shows (British and Russian), concerts and dances were arranged at the International Club, most of the survivors appeared unable to shake themselves out of their lethargy, and they spent much of their time lying in bed or aimlessly walking about the town. The Base Chaplain, The Reverend F. H. Outram, R.N.V.R.,* did splendid work amongst them under very difficult conditions by running a library and a daily news sheet, and arranging games and sports. He recalls that at the start they had one football, and in an unguarded moment this was purloined by some local youths. ' After that we had to content ourselves with sports meetings.' The impromptu concerts caused some interest amongst the Russian welfare personnel, and he speaks highly of one of them, Tatiana Gorinova, who was most co-operative. Besides holding Sunday services, he also ran a confirmation class for British and American sailors, and gave them letters to take to any Bishop whom they might meet on their return to civilisation. Many wrote to him subsequently, and one American, now married and with a married daughter, still writes to him every Christmas.

The officer survivors were quartered in the Intourist Hotel where, in fact, they fared little better

* Now Dean of Battle

D

than the men and where they had more than their
fair share of bed bugs.   Several rooms in which
furniture and fittings seemed to be infested had to
be evacuated.

If the conditions for the fit were tough, those for
the sick were even more so.   After being removed
from the Sevroles Hospital in which they were at
first accommodated, they were divided between
Military Hospitals Nos 191 and 2524.   Each ward
contained sixteen to twenty beds in a cubic space
far less than that found in even the worst of British
hospitals, the beds being about two feet apart.
They were hard but fairly clean.   There were rooms
set aside for surgical dressings, and a physiotherapy
department in charge of a capable doctor.   The X-
ray department was greatly handicapped by a complete lack of film, so pictures could only be screened,
and it was necessary to rely on the diagnostic capa-
bilities of a radiographer who did not inspire confidence.   There was a total lack of aseptic technique
and analgesic treatment.   Procedures for achieving
anaesthesia were also poor, and most cases were
operated on under local anaesthetics.   Wound infec-
tion was the rule rather than the exception.   Technique in the operating theatre could only be described
as ' non-sterile '.   Rubber gloves were unobtainable,
and when Dr Wilkins presented two pairs to Professor Orloff of the Archangel School of Medicine
' he was overcome with gratitude '.   The British
Medical Officers did their best to make good the
Russian deficiencies in drugs such as morphia, novo-
caine and sulphanilamide tablets and powders, but

it was only by using great diplomacy that they were able to overcome the Russian political objections which forbade them to admit to the lack of any medical supplies.

Food in the hospitals was poor, and patients obliged to remain in them for any length of time rapidly became emaciated. As there was only one diet available, those who should have had special diets had to make the best of it. Added to all these problems was that of the language difficulty which prevented the patients from making the nursing staff understand their most pressing bodily requirements. The situation was later improved when the services of a Russian girl interpreter were obtained.

The plight of these unfortunate survivors from Convoy PQ17 was reported to the Admiralty and the Ministry of War Transport, and urgent consultations were held in London to decide what more could be done for them. There was no question of running another convoy to Russia, nor of bringing one back until the days of continuous daylight came to an end. During the last week of July four destroyers were sent to Archangel with ammunition to replace the large quantity which had been expended, especially by the A.A. Ships and the Rescue Ships, but they had little room for carrying stocks of food which were so badly needed. It was finally agreed that the United States cruiser *Tuscaloosa,* then attached to the Home Fleet, accompanied by three destroyers, one British and two American, should be sent to Murmansk. The cruiser carried three hundred tons and each of the destroyers forty tons of stores, and it was hoped that this would ease the strain until repatriation became possible. The *Tuscaloosa* also carried a small hospital unit which had been urgently requested. The force sailed from the Clyde on 13th August and reached its destination without incident.

It had been agreed that on their return home the warships should bring as many hospital cases as they could accommodate. At Archangel there were one hundred and sixteen deserving cases; thirty-five had been brought round from Murmansk. They had been in Russian hospitals since March, and because of poor food, and the constant bombing they had experienced, they were in a poor state. The majority of the cases had immersion foot and many had lost two or more limbs. Some had been sunk and rescued twice. Yet despite the suffering they had endured, most of them kept remarkably cheerful, their constant inquiry when visited by the British Medical Officers being ' When are we going home ? ' The arrangements had to be kept secret for as long as possible, and it was not until 21st August that the hospital authorities were told of the impending move. As can be imagined, the news that at long last some were to be repatriated caused tremendous elation amongst those who had been named, coupled with intense anxiety lest there should be a last-minute hitch and something unforeseen should happen to interfere with their departure.

Thirty patients were selected for passage to Murmansk and were embarked in the minesweeper *Salamander*, which had formed part of the escort of the

ill-fated Convoy PQ17. Russian doctors and nurses
came down to the quayside to see them off and a
remarkable farewell scene took place in which tears
and kisses were much in evidence. Whatever may
have been the failings of the Russian medical services at that time due to shortage of drugs and
equipment, in kindness and warmheartedness they
excelled themselves. This was the unanimous
opinion of the British Medical Officers who had
dealings with them.

There had been air raids on Archangel during the
two nights prior to sailing, and in view of this evidence of enemy activity and the pent-up feelings of
the patients, all were given a sedative during their
first night on board. Doctors Wilkins, MacBain
and McCallum accompanied them to Murmansk,
which was reached in two days without enemy
interference.

But there was a final ordeal in store for these
much-tried men—one of those administrative muddles
which seem to occur at the most inopportune moments. On arrival in the Kola Inlet, orders were
received from the Senior British Naval Officer,
North Russia, that instead of embarking in the
Tuscaloosa the patients were to be landed at Vaenga,
a town on the inlet a few miles from Murmansk,
and accommodated in the Russian hospital there.
The effect of this news on the men was ' nothing
short of pitiful ' wrote Dr MacBain. But after the
last case had been taken away and put to bed, the
order was countermanded. While the patients were
being transferred to the cruiser an air raid took

place, but the ' hundred guns ' went into action and the enemy was driven off. Dr MacBain and his sick-berth attendant Bryant, who had supported him so well in all the vicissitudes which they had endured since the *Zaafaran* was sunk, returned home in the cruiser. Doctors Wilkins and McCallum went back to their ships at Archangel, to find that during their absence there had been an air raid in which a lot of medical stores had been destroyed. An interesting account of the event is contained in a letter which the resourceful Mr Wolf subsequently wrote to Dr MacBain. ' After your departure . . . within three days Jerry came over and very nicely sorted out your pet sick bay which was burned completely down. About a hundred of us rushed up from the Intourist and although the building was well alight, we managed to stop the fire spreading by pulling down the neighbouring junk shed, at the same time salvaging the survivors' stores and all those medical stores which had been set aside for that reason. Only the stores in the sick bay itself were destroyed, the two big chests were burnt out. . . . Some of the more valuable tablets were also saved.' Had it not been for Dr MacBain's foresight, there is no doubt that the situation would have been worse.

During air raid alerts the British doctors went to the hospitals to help evacuate the patients from the top floors in an attempt to boost their morale. But in their crippled state, and surrounded by strangers, this was not easily accomplished. ' We had a couple of blitzes, H.E.'s, etc. there,' continued Mr Wolf, ' and by the time we eventually left there was quite a bit of damage in places. Severus was blown inside out with numerous H.E. blasts, the Museum Karl Marx or near by and generally round that quarter.'

The rest of the survivors, the crews of the now unloaded merchant ships and those of the *Rathlin* and *Zamalek*, had to wait until mid-September before their stay in North Russia came to an end. Food in the ships was running low, and on board the *Zamalek*, in which Mr Wolf took passage, their diet consisted of ' corned beef, corned-beef pie, corned-beef pudding, corned-beef soup, etc., *ad lib.*, with ship's biscuits and one whole slice of bread per person per day. No potatoes or vegetables, and of course we gradually got crowded out with more victims [*sic*] all the time coming home.' Captain Morris remarked, ' Everybody fully appreciated the position and there were no complaints.'

From a medical point of view the bitterest blow was the Russian veto on landing the hospital unit, for on the arrival of this great store had been set. This was yet another instance of Russian pride, and their unwillingness to admit the inadequacy of their own medical service. They willingly accepted the supplies which accompanied the unit, but it was not until the matter was taken up by Mr Churchill personally with Stalin that the veto was withdrawn, and the unit was allowed to land. By that time the emergency was less acute, as the greater part of the survivors had been repatriated.

6

The Comeback

IT had been the practice for the outward convoy to, and the homeward convoy from, North Russia to sail simultaneously. This meant that the two crossed halfway through the voyage, and this enabled the Home Fleet to provide cover simultaneously for both convoys. However, in view of the disaster which had overtaken PQ17, new tactics were evolved. It was decided to give the next convoy to Russia, PQ18, a very powerful escort of destroyers and, most important of all, an escort carrier which would accompany the convoy all the way to Kanin Noss at the entrance to the White Sea. Here the escort would transfer to the homeward-bound Convoy QP14.

There was, unfortunately, only one Rescue Ship available for PQ18. This was the *Copeland* which, under her Master, Captain J. McKellar, O.B.E., had already made a name for herself by her efficiency and good work with the Atlantic and Gibraltar convoys. She had been thoroughly fitted out for a winter passage to the Arctic. All cabins and accommodation had extra steam heaters installed. Water tanks and pipes had been heavily insulated, and the hull had been strengthened against encounter with ice. Finally, all the officers and men had been issued with sets of Arctic clothing.

As Captain McKellar was due for some well-earned leave, his place was taken by his First Mate, W. G. Hartley, who was promoted Master. He proved himself in every way equal to the new responsibilities with which he was charged. The Chief Engineer was W. McPherson; he had been with *Copeland* since before she began work as a Rescue Ship. The Medical Officer was Surgeon Lieutenant-Commander W. H. C. M. Hamilton, R.N. On joining in his naval uniform in January 1941 he had been told by Captain McKellar: " All you need for this ship is a peaked cap and a sports jacket." The Chief Radio Operator was Mr Horace Bell, a veteran of the First World War; with his permission extensive quotations have been made from his hitherto unpublished account of the voyage.

The *Copeland* sailed with the convoy from Loch Ewe on 2nd September 1942, and on clearing the Minches it encountered the full force of an Atlantic gale, which impeded progress and scattered the ships. However, *Copeland* carried on, and after two days of severe buffeting reached the harbour of Reykjavik. There she waited for the convoy to re-assemble. This accomplished, the whole body set out again and shaped course for its destination, Archangel. It comprised forty ships and was the largest convoy yet to sail on the Arctic route.

Although German reconnaissance aircraft located PQ18 late on 8th September, they lost it again due to low cloud. But it was also being trailed by U-

D 2

boats.   For a time these were kept at a distance by the carrier's anti-submarine aircraft.   Then on 12th September the enemy aircraft regained touch, and on that morning two U-boats managed to get through the screen and torpedo the Russian ship *Stalingrad* and the American *Oliver Elsworth*.   The *Copeland* was quickly on the scene rescuing survivors, and she was assisted by some motor minesweepers which were on passage for transfer to the Soviet Navy.

That afternoon the expected air attacks began. Except for quotations which are attributed to other writers, those which follow in this chapter are from Horace Bell's record.   ' The ceiling was round about 3,000 feet, very overcast, sea moderate, fresh breeze, cold and occasional falls of sleet and snow, visibility poor, but as soon as a plane dipped below the clouds, he found a burst or two near enough to send him in again.'   The enemy was biding his time.   Then at last he struck.   ' A wave of torpedo bombers was seen approaching, followed by another—and another, but it was really just one continuous attack and was over in less time than it takes to tell.   We could watch the whole thing, and it was a most amazing sight.   They came in low on the starboard bow of the convoy and seemed to fill the whole horizon. They swept in, thirty-five to forty of them, about twenty feet above sea level, disregarding completely the escort screen ; it was the merchant ships they were after, and the merchant ships they meant to get.   As they came within range, every available gun opened up on them, and in a matter of seconds we had a really good barrage going, but still they came on. A pall of smoke hung like a curtain out on the starboard flank of the convoy, criss-crossed by the bright red tracks of the tracers and punctuated by the flashes of the shell bursts. The place was an absolute inferno. Every plane as it emerged from the haze became the target for the smaller weapons too, few of them could have come through without damage of some sort, but they were undeterred. Each one, as it got into position, dropped two torpedoes, banked and swept off astern—fast wicked-looking monoplanes—a few on fire, but there was no time to follow them and see whether they crashed.'

Due either to not seeing the flags or to misunderstanding the Commodore's emergency signal to alter course together to comb the tracks of the torpedoes, the two starboard columns of the convoy turned in succession, and six of the seven ships were hit. One of these, loaded with explosives, disintegrated. 'There wasn't a tremendous lot of noise—just a huge column of smoke and dull red flame, lighting up the whole sky for a few seconds, and then silence. Everyone seemed momentarily stunned or fascinated, watching the smoke billow upwards. Of the ship not a trace remained.'

For the next hour or so the *Copeland* was busy picking up survivors from the other five ships. One of them, the *Empire Beaumont*, had a lucky escape insomuch as she was hit in number four hold, the only one which did not contain explosives. Amongst the survivors were two Russians, Colonel Toman and his wife, who got away in a boat.

By the time the *Copeland* had collected all the survivors, who now totalled one hundred and sixty-three, the convoy was several miles to the eastward, and because of the number of submarines which had been reported round the convoy, her position was not an enviable one. Captain Hartley set off at his best speed to regain his station. He left behind him the blazing wreck of the *Empire Beaumont*, thankful that she did not blow up while he was in her vicinity. While overhauling the convoy, the *Copeland* was attacked by two torpedo bombers evidently looking for an easy victim. They came in from astern and dropped two torpedoes, which Captain Hartley managed to avoid by putting his helm hard over at the right moment. 'It was in rather subdued state of mind that we resumed our normal station. We had lost ten ships that day, most of them inside five minutes, and had another four, five or even six days to go before reaching port and comparative safety.'

The air attacks continued intermittently until dark. At 2.26 a.m. on 14th September U-457 managed to get in an attack and torpedo the freighting tanker *Atheltemplar* in the engine-room. She was carrying fuel oil which did not ignite, but the loss of this valuable cargo was a blow to the Russians, for whom it was intended.

The convoy steamed on. 'We had Queenies (U-boats) to port and starboard, and Bandits (enemy aircraft) were gathering round.' But it was not until the afternoon that the air attacks were renewed. Once more the air was filled with radio-telephonic chatter. 'JU 88s approaching—Heinkel 115s in sector Robert—Keep your eyes open—High-level

bombers expected over any minute now—Eight
JU 88s—no ten at least—diving on port wing of
convoy now—Own fighters port bow of convoy—
six, seven, eight, nine torpedo bombers ahead of the
convoy—low down—give me a bearing someone—
at least twenty of them coming in ahead—keep your
eyes on them—there's a hell of a lot of them—and
so on.' This time the enemy was concentrating on
the carrier, which was steaming into the wind, her
fighter aircraft taking off as fast as they could be
launched and tearing into the attackers with guns
blazing. ' I happened to be watching that sector as
the planes flew in. The leader came in to about
three hundred yards from one ship before dropping
his torpedoes and then swept on down the column.
As he passed the gunner raked him fore and aft and
bright tongues of flame flickered from his starboard
engine. He dipped, recovered, dipped again and
seemed just about to crash, when his torpedoes
reached their mark and the ship simply vanished
into thin air. As for the plane it broke up into small
pieces like a well-shot clay pigeon.' The ship which
had been hit was an American, the *Mary Luchenback*.
Like most of the ships in the convoy, she was loaded
with explosives. Once again the onlookers had to
witness the horrifying spectacle of a ship blowing up.
' In the stupefying moments of silence and inactivity
that followed, we watched as an enormous column
of smoke billowed upwards, slow, thick, black and
ugly—no flame this time, just smoke, up and up till
it reached the clouds. Gradually, from the overhanging top, there drifted down dust—like a shower

of rain, and that was all. There was no tremendous report, just a deep awful rumble.'

The air attacks lasted for almost three hours. Then the sky became overcast and the enemy withdrew, giving the defenders a welcome respite. On board the *Copeland*, in which the survivors numbered two hundred and fourteen and her crew seventy-one, anxiety prevailed. The boats and rafts could accommodate perhaps a third of the total, so it would be a grim business if she were hit. However, that evening a destroyer, H.M.S. *Martin*, came alongside and took off British and American survivors for return to Iceland. This left ninety-six survivors in the *Copeland*, of whom eighty-seven were Russians, two Czech, six British and two American cot cases.

On 15th September cloud persisted, and although the enemy was out again in force looking for the convoy only occasional attacks, mostly by single aircraft, took place, and no ships were hit. ' It was a lovely " coorse " day, wind and rain, sleet and snow showers, and we got progressively happier as we got further and further away from the Norwegian bases.' But the enemy had not yet given up, and there were still a dozen U-boats in contact with the convoy.

On the evening of the 16th, the transfer of forces from PQ18 to the returning QP14 took place. ' We turned south skirting down the coast of Novaya Zemlya. The weather became less cold ; we began to settle down to our usual routine and forget the bad times behind us. The Russian survivors were settling down and our anxiety with regard to them lessened. Some had been in bad shape when they came aboard—two at least had not a stitch of clothing on and one poor devil was almost out of his mind. His wife and two-day-old child were in his ship when it was hit; the infant was lost, but his wife survived with her ribs crushed and after being in the icy water for quite a time.'

But on 18th September the all-too-familiar alarm bells sounded again. The Germans wanted a better return than nine ships for the thirty-four aircraft they had lost. At 8.20 a.m. a force of twelve Heinkel 111 torpedo aircraft attacked. ' *Copeland* at this time was lying pretty far back in the second (port) column. We thought it was all up with us as ten Torpedo aircraft swept in skimming the water, divided just astern of us and roared past on either side, dropping their fish as they went by. We could see them leaping clean out of the water like tarpon before settling down on their course.' With guns firing and the ship twisting and turning under helm, *Copeland* managed to dodge the torpedoes, but an American ship, the *Kentucky*, was hit. She did not sink, and there was some hope of saving her until an hour later a bombing attack took place and she received a hit which sealed her fate.

Even after the convoy entered the White Sea, the enemy kept up his attacks and, as if that was not enough, a full gale sprang up during the afternoon of the 19th and prevented the pilots from taking the ships across the Dvina bar. The night was foul, with a snow-laden wind. The American *Campfire* and several other ships ran aground. There were two more air raids on the 20th. Happily these were

unsuccessful, being repulsed by Russian fighters.
But it was not until 7 a.m. on the 21st that the *Copeland* secured to Krasnaya Quay at Archangel. A
finishing touch to this voyage was given by one of
the Russian lady survivors. When taking her leave,
she said in halting English : " I thank you, Captain
Hartley, your officers and men of this ship for your
good fight and for your kindness to me. Good luck
to you and your country."

Although the comments of the Russian Commander-in-Chief, Northern Fleet, Admiral Golovko
in his war memoirs are often wide of the mark, those
on PQ18 are more apposite : ' Such then, are the
results of the September Convoy PQ18. They con-
firm once more that given resolute action by covering
forces and adequate preliminary combat measures,
the enemy's surface ships can be neutralised, while
the attacks of U-boats and aircraft can be repulsed
—and with heavy loss to the enemy—by a correctly
organised order of battle.' *   It had indeed been a
hard battle, and thirteen of the forty ships had been
lost ; but it did much to restore the image which
PQ17 had destroyed.

While PQ18 was fighting its way into port, QP14,
consisting of fifteen ships, mostly survivors from
PQ17, and the Rescue Ships *Rathlin* and *Zamalek*,
was ploughing steadily westwards through the Barents Sea, unaware that the German High Command
had planned its destruction by some of their surface
ships. But the opposition put up by the formidable escort on the outward voyage encouraged

---

* *With The Red Fleet*, p. 180

second thoughts, and the surface operation was called off.

The *Rathlin* had embarked fourteen of the patients remaining in Russian hospitals. Nearly all were cases of immersion foot who had undergone various amputations, and three were completely helpless cases in cots in the Sick Bay. The *Rathlin* also carried forty-eight survivors and three Russian women. In the *Zamalek* were another fifteen cases from the Russian hospitals. The ship's hospital had a complement of Dutch sailors from the *Paulus Potter*, sunk on 5th July four hundred and fifty miles to the west of Novaya Zemlya. They were big men, and all were suffering from frostbite. Every time Action Stations sounded they had to be helped to gain the upper deck, as they would have been helpless if caught between decks. The *Zamalek* also had on board a sailor from the Free French corvette *La Malouine*. He had broken his leg playing football, and it had been set in plaster with a walking calliper to make him mobile. When Dr McCallum jokingly pointed out that it would help him to float upright, he ruefully replied, "*Oui, Docteur, mais a quelle profondeur?*" The remainder of the survivors were distributed amongst ships of the convoy.

Fog shielded the convoy for the first three days of its passage, but the bitter cold and snow squalls hampered the operation of the carrier's anti-submarine aircraft and made it easier for the U-boats to trail the ships. On 20th September they managed to claim their first victim; in the early hours of the morning they torpedoed the minesweeper H.M.S.

Leda, mistaking her for a destroyer. The *Rothlin* turned back to pick up survivors, but was forestalled by the trawlers *Northern Gem* and *Seagull,* which were near by. *Northern Gem* subsequently transferred to the Rescue Ship thirty-three survivors whom she had rescued, including one with severe burns who had swum half a mile in the icy water. While this operation was in progress, information was received that the Master of the American ship *Samuel Chase* had developed acute appendicitis. The *Rathlin* closed the ship and took him off, at the same time obtaining some flour, of which she was desperately short. No sooner had the rescue motorboat been hoisted than U-255 put three torpedoes into the American *Silver Sword,* a ship which had escaped destruction in PQ17. The *Rathlin* picked up fifty-five survivors and a dog from boats and rafts, and the *Zamalek* a further nine men. *Zamalek* was still suffering from the effects of the severe battering she had received from enemy bombing, and she could make only eight knots. Also her fuel consumption had greatly increased, so her value as a Rescue Ship was impaired.

Later that day the U-boats scored another success, when U-703 torpedoed the destroyer H.M.S. *Somali.* But it was two days later, on 22nd September, that they delivered their most successful attack, torpedoing the Royal Fleet Auxiliary tanker *Gray Ranger,* the American ship *Bellingham,* and the British ship *Ocean Voice,* in which the indomitable Commodore Dowding had hoisted his broad pennant. The two Rescue Ships dropped astern to rescue survivors, the *Rathlin* picking up twenty-six from the *Belling-ham*, her companion in so much adversity, and thirty-three from the *Gray Ranger*. *Rathlin* now had on board two hundred and eighty-one survivors, and the food situation was acute. On board the *Ocean Voice* there was a Russian trade delegation, and three days after sailing one of the lady delegates had given birth. When the first torpedo struck, the baby was put in a suitcase, but the second torpedo shattered the accommodation and it was not seen again. The *Zamalek* rescued eighty-five survivors, including eight women and eleven children, of whom three were babies under a year old. Commodore Dowding and his staff, who were amongst the last to leave the sinking ship, were picked up by one of the escorts.

Enemy aircraft continued to shadow the convoy to within seventy miles of Iceland, but the U-boats were called off after their triple success. Before the much-tried ships and their survivors reached port they had to endure the buffeting of a severe northerly gale. The *Rathlin* and the *Zamalek* put into the Icelandic port of Seydisfiord to replenish with much-needed provisions and stores, which enabled 'all on board to have their first decent meal for over two months. They reached the Clyde on the afternoon of 27th September after an absence of over three months.

During the whole of the voyage Dr Wilkins was kept busy attending to the patients embarked at Archangel and the injured survivors picked up *en route*. He was assisted by eight D.E.M.S. ratings, survivors from ships which had been sunk, who

volunteered for duty as additional sick-berth attendants, an extremely valuable service which they performed with great success. Six major operations
were performed, and one patient suffering from two
gangrenous immersion feet certainly owed his life
to the skilful attention which he received.

' The safe arrival of twenty-seven ships in PQ18
and the return of fourteen ships in QP14 after such
powerful and protracted opposition is a great achievement which redounds greatly to the credit of all who
planned and took part in the operation,' signalled the
Admiralty on 27th September 1942. ' The Prime
Minister wishes to associate himself with this message.'

Both Captain Banning and Captain Morris were
awarded the Distinguished Service Order, and Captain McGowan of the *Zaafaran* the Distinguished
Service Cross, for their bravery and devotion to
duty. They also received Lloyd's Medals and
Commendations. Several other officers and men of
the Rescue Ships received decorations and awards.

Because it was once again found necessary to sus-
pend the Arctic convoys, this time because of the
Allied invasion of North Africa, the *Copeland* was
obliged to spend six weeks in Archangel. To express their thanks for the arrival of the ships of PQ18
the Russian authorities arranged a banquet to which
representatives of both naval and merchant ships
were invited. Despite the abject poverty which was
so plainly evident all around, the fare provided was
lavish. ' The tables were loaded with mounds of

caviare, red and black; large platters of butter sculped in wonderful designs, flags, flowers, etc., were a feature of each table. At frequent intervals there were groups of bottles of champagne, vodka, red and white wines, which were replaced from time to time by others.' A number of English-speaking Russian girls, all dressed alike in the regulation white blouse and black skirt, had been assembled to act as hostesses. They proved excellent conversationalists, until asked questions. Then they found the utmost difficulty in understanding. The meal, in true Russian tradition, was gargantuan — soup, fish, poultry, meats, sorbets, sweets, ice-cream—and the hostesses made it their business to see that a glass was never allowed to remain empty. ' There was a break halfway through the meal to allow some circulation between tables, blank spaces to be refilled, and contacts to be established between friends. I was heartily embraced by a Russian with a three-day growth of beard on his chin. He turned out to be one of *Copeland*'s survivors, to whom I had apparently been of some small service.'

In addition to bands, singers, ballet, choirs and dancers on a stage at one end of the hall, there were speeches from the Russian Admiral and Heroes of the Soviet Union from a dais at the other, the two sometimes competing with one another for the attention of the guests. The banquet lasted for seven hours, ' but on emerging from the hall we were considerably sobered by the sight of the usual pathetic crowd outside, begging for bread.'

A large number of empty ships had now accumulated in the White Sea ports, and to avoid the loss of their services for six months if they became frozen in, the Admiralty decided to run a special convoy to bring them home. It sailed on 17th November and comprised twenty-eight ships, and the *Copeland*. The enemy got wind of its departure and planned to use surface ships to attack it, but a spell of really bad weather frustrated his design. In the event the convoy became scattered and the *Copeland* made the passage almost alone. ' There was nothing we could do, so we just plugged on in heavy seas, as one black day followed a blacker and more depressing night. In the end, and all unbelieving, we sighted Iceland.'

The Rescue Ships *Copeland*, *Rathlin* and *Zamalek* subsequently sailed in a total of ten outward and nine homeward convoys to and from North Russia. During one of these voyages the *Rathlin*, in charge of a local pilot, went aground in Molotovsk and badly damaged her rudder. As a result she missed the return convoy. The Master had visions of being frozen in for the winter, as the mishap occurred in late August 1944. However, the Russians rose to the occasion. The ship was trimmed by the head to raise her stern out of water and a raft built round it. By this means repairs were made in a month and she was able to return home in company with the *Zamalek*, in Convoy RA60. The presence of two Rescue Ships in this convoy was fortunate, as two ships were torpedoed simultaneously, and the *Rathlin* was able to rescue fifty-seven survivors from one while the *Zamalek* was picking up sixty-seven from the other. But never again were the fierce battles of 1942 to be repeated, though until the heavy ships *Tirpitz* and *Scharnhorst* were sunk the threat to these convoys remained serious, and right up to the end of the war the U-boats continued to take their toll of the British and American merchant ships bringing aid to Russia.

7

Those Invaluable Vessels

IN an attempt to placate the Russians for the suspension of the Arctic convoys, the experiment was tried of sailing ships independently from Iceland to North Russia with volunteer crews. To provide accommodation for those members of a crew who were unwilling to take part in this hazardous enterprise, the Ministry of War Transport sent the Rescue Ships *Rathlin* and *Toward* to Iceland at the end of October 1942 to act as accommodation vessels. This was a grave misuse of these valuable ships, and they were not really suitable for the purpose intended. It can only be explained by the very high priority accorded to the experiment, which in the event proved to be a costly failure.* Admittedly the losses in the Atlantic in the autumn of 1942 had not been quite as heavy as those during the summer, but ships were still being sunk at an average rate of three a day and, as will be seen, there were never enough Rescue Ships to meet the demand.

On 18th December, the *Toward*, Master Captain G. K. Hudson, having been released from her base-ship duties in Iceland, sailed from the Clyde with the escort of Convoy ONS154. When eight days

* See *The Russian Convoys* (Schofield), p. 127

out, she picked up numerous bearings of U-boats, and it soon became apparent that a concerted attack was about to be launched on the convoy.

Just after midnight on 27th December, distress rockets were observed from the direction of the starboard wing of the convoy, and Captain Hudson steamed towards them. He first came across survivors from the British ship *Melrose Abbey* (not to be confused with the Rescue Ship of that name) and rescued twenty-six men from lifeboats and rafts. A second torpedoed ship, the S.S. *Empire Union*, yielded sixty-three survivors. Next he located the Dutch ship *Soekaboeni* in a sinking condition, and picked up fifty-one members of her crew. Proceeding to rejoin the convoy, the *Toward* came across lifeboats from the British ship *King Edward*, another victim of the attack, and picked up twenty-three more survivors. The Senior Officer of the escort had detailed a corvette to screen the *Toward* during these rescue operations, and this was a wise precaution appreciated by all on board the Rescue Ship, now numbering 163.

Further attacks were made on the convoy on the night of 28th December, and six more ships were torpedoed. But because the *Toward* was fully loaded with survivors, the Commodore of the convoy had ordered Captain Hudson not to take part in any further rescue operations. The burden of rescuing survivors from the six ships therefore fell on the escorts, to the inevitable detriment of their offensive potential against the attacking U-boats.

The loss of the *Zaafaran* was especially unfortunate,

as she was one of the three oil-burning ships in
the Rescue Fleet, and it was not until the end of
September 1942 that a replacement was found for
her. This was the *St Sunniva*, a vessel belonging to
the North of Scotland, Orkney and Shetlands Steamship Company. She was on the small side, displacing
only 1,368 gross tons, but by virtue of the service
for which she had been built, she had ample passenger accommodation amidships and a large dining
saloon aft capable of seating two hundred people,
both factors in her favour as a Rescue Ship. She
was sent to Hull, where the work of conversion was
carried out ; this included fitting additional bunker
and water stowage to enable her to make Atlantic
crossings.

It was most appropriate that Captain McGowan,
D.S.C., one of the most experienced of the Rescue
Ship Masters, should be appointed to command her,
and he took with him many of the officers and men
who had served under him in the *Zaafaran*. On the
way round from Hull to the Clyde at the end of
December, he expressed himself well satisfied with
the way in which his new command had stood up to
the very heavy weather encountered off the north
coast of Scotland.

The winter of 1942/43 was an exceptionally bitter
and stormy one in the North Atlantic, and on 3rd
January 1943 Captain McGowan took the *St Sunniva*
to sea on her first voyage as a Rescue Ship, escorting
a convoy bound for Halifax. It is known that very
heavy weather was encountered during the passage,
but the Rescue Ship must have survived this, since

she was sighted off Sable Island, one hundred and sixty miles east of Halifax, on 23rd January. What happened to her after that can only be surmised. The fact that a ship in the same convoy reached Halifax on 22nd January coated with ice varying from three to ten feet thick suggests that the *St Sunniva* may have been similarly affected and that she capsized as a result of the extra weight on her upperworks. No radio message was received to provide a clue as to the cause of her loss with all hands, an exceptionally cruel blow in view of the devoted service rendered by her Master and crew, who had been instrumental in saving two hundred and twenty lives in their former ship the *Zaafaran*. Amongst those lost was the Chief Radio Officer Mr C. Wolf, whose resource and initiative had been of such great value in North Russia.

But there was even worse to come. On 27th January 1943 the *Toward* began her homeward voyage from Halifax as part of the escort of Convoy SC118. The sailing of this convoy had been compromised both by German radio intelligence and by a survivor from a tanker torpedoed in a previous convoy and rescued by a U-boat. The prisoner had confirmed that a slow convoy was following two days behind that in which his ship had been sailing. In consequence, the enemy concentrated all available U-boats in an attempt to intercept. Even so the convoy passed through the enemy patrol line unseen, and it might not have been attacked had it not been for the accidental firing of a snowflake rocket from the S.S. *Annik* on the night of 3rd February. When

the brilliant flare burst overhead it was seen by a
U-boat which immediately transmitted the information to the rest of her group. The *Toward* obtained
a bearing of this transmission on her HF/DF
equipment, and so was able to warn the Senior
Officer of the escort force of the likelihood of an
attack.

For the next three days a furious battle raged
round the convoy, but the only casualty was a straggler. Moreover, the U-boats got a very rough
handling and retired to lick their wounds. On 6th
February the *Toward*'s Medical Officer, Surgeon
Lieutenant Glennie, R.N.V.R., transferred in bad
weather to the S.S. *Celtic Star*, to attend to a man
who had fallen off the mast and severely injured
himself. The doctor decided that the patient must
be brought back to the Rescue Ship to be properly
looked after. By the time the transfer was complete
the *Toward* had fallen some twenty miles astern of
the convoy; she set out at her best speed to rejoin
it.

Meanwhile the attackers had been reinforced by
one of the crack U-boat commanders, Baron von
Forstner, who had orders to rally the battered group
and renew the attack. On the night of 7th February,
shortly before midnight, he led the U-boats back.
It so happened that the starboard side of the convoy
was uncovered as he approached, the escorts having
sensed that another attack was imminent and moved
out to meet it. The *Toward* was just resuming her
station in the convoy when Forstner fired his first
torpedo at what he took to be a small freighter. It

struck the *Toward* on the port side just forward of the bridge. The usual distress signals were fired and radio message despatched, but she quickly developed a heavy list and Captain Hudson ordered ' Abandon ship '. The weather at the time was bad, and although the boats got away several of them were swamped and capsized. An escort vessel came to the rescue, but out of a total crew of seventy-two and two medical cases embarked, only one officer, Mr G. L. Campbell, and fifteen men were saved.

The loss of the Rescue Ship was a disaster in itself, and an even bigger one so far as the convoy was concerned. A few hours later the United States troopship *Mallory*, carrying four hundred and fifteen Service personnel in addition to her crew of eighty-one, straggled, was torpedoed and sank. Of her company only two hundred and thirty-four were rescued. Five more ships were lost from the convoy, and many of their crews went to swell the total of lives lost during that tragic voyage. Captain Hudson was a fine seaman and a great loss to the Rescue Fleet, but his spirit lived on. Witness the way in which the survivors of his crew volunteered at once for service in other Rescue Ships. Mr Campbell, after being First Officer of the *Goodwin*, eventually became Master of the *Rathlin*. In this ship he made four trips to North Russia, and was awarded the O.B.E. for his splendid service.

Less than three weeks after the loss of the *Toward*, the *Stockport* was sunk. The loss of three Rescue Ships in so short a space of time lent urgency to the need to find replacements for them. On 16th

February 1943 the Admiralty asked the Head of the British Admiralty Delegation in Washington to investigate the possibility of obtaining suitable ships from the United States Navy. The U.S. Coastguard Cutters would have been valuable additions to the Rescue Fleet, but all were employed on escort duties. Ten of them had been turned over to the Royal Navy in 1941 ; the remainder had been pressed into service with the United States Navy to make good the latter's serious shortage of coastal escort vessels. The U.S. Navy Department offered to consider the construction of eleven wooden ships suitable for rescue work, but the pressure on American shipyards for every type of ship, from carriers to landing craft, as well as for merchant ships to replace the tonnage being sunk, was so great that nothing came of the offer, despite the fact that many United States ships were being sunk in the Atlantic and Arctic convoys. The Director of the Trade Division, when he was in Washington in April 1943, took the matter up with the well-known American industrialist, Mr Henry Kaiser, who had earned a reputation for rapid ship construction. But on learning that the demand was for only thirty of these ships, he confessed that while he was most sympathetic it was not a big enough job for him to tackle.*

On 2nd January 1943, the day before the *St Sunniva* sailed from the Clyde on her last voyage, the veteran Rescue Ship *Accrington*, Master Captain A. W. R. M. Greenham, was escorting a homeward-bound convoy. At 2.15 a.m. a distress signal was

---

* See *British Sea Power* (Schofield), p. 196

seen astern of the convoy. On turning back to investigate, Captain Greenham found the American ship *J. Van Rensselaer* blazing furiously from stem to stern as a result of having been torpedoed. It was blowing hard and a mountainous sea was running, but eight survivors were rescued from one of the ship's boats, and soon afterwards two rafts were encountered. To these, eighteen exhausted men were clinging. They were quite unable to save themselves, so Captain Greenham put his ship alongside and two of his men, Able Seamen McIntyre and Thomson, went over the side, boarded the rafts and secured lines round each man in turn. The survivors were then hauled up. Unfortunately two were found to be dead, and a third died later on board the Rescue Ship.

The search for further survivors went on for several hours without success. The fire in the wreck now appeared to be dying down, and returning to have a final look Captain Greenham observed one man still on board. He sent the rescue motorboat across for him, and in it went the Second Engineer to see if there were any chance of saving the ship. This proved to be impossible, and she was later sunk by an escort vessel. Altogether the *Accrington* spent fourteen hours in the area. On the afternoon of the following day a strange object was sighted. This turned out to be the forward half of a torpedoed tanker, floating vertically, with a man perched on the stem. The rescue boat was launched, but before it reached the wreck the man fell off into the sea. On being picked up he was found to have died several hours previously. In the opinion of the Medical Officer he had probably frozen to death on his bleak perch, and had been dislodged by an extra violent lurch of the wreck.

One of the most remarkable rescues of that stormy winter was made by the Rescue Ship *Melrose Abbey*, Master Captain R. Good, O.B.E. The outward voyage to Halifax, which began at the end of January 1943, was comparatively uneventful apart from the bad weather and bitter cold. During a lull in the gale a sick man from the S.S. *Bruce* was transferred to the Rescue Ship, but the cold was so intense that the boat's crew which was sent for him suffered severely. The homeward voyage began on 25th February, and this was notable both for winds of near hurricane force and for a series of rescues made under exceptionally adverse conditions.

At 5.25 p.m. on 9th March Captain Good sighted white rockets being fired off his starboard bow, and a second or two later he received a radio report that the American ship *Malantic* had been torpedoed. It was blowing hard from the west, with occasional snow squalls of gale force and a high sea running. Reaching the scene of the disaster, one man was seen in the water. While he was being picked up, a lifeboat was sighted to windward. In the darkness the boat mistook the Rescue Ship for a submarine, and began to pull away from her. The boat contained eleven men, including the Master, who had been injured by the explosion of the torpedoes. The *Melrose Abbey* closed the lifeboat, and her crew rescued the Master and nine of the boat's occupants.

ZAMALEK *on arrival at Halifax, Nova Scotia, in January 1943*

Captain J. L. Davidson with members of ACCRINGTON'S *Ship-Company*

The eleventh man, who had attended to the securing of the boat, was so exhausted by his efforts that when his turn came he lost his balance and fell into the sea. Although one of the ship's officers went in after him and nearly lost his own life in so doing, the man disappeared.

The survivors now on board informed Captain Good that in the vicinity was another lifeboat, containing the remainder of the *Malantic*'s crew, so a search was begun for it. The weather had meanwhile deteriorated further, the squalls being even more violent, and charged with sleet and snow. This, added to the darkness, made the task of locating the lifeboat extremely difficult, but eventually it was found. It was completely water-logged and the men in it were wet, frozen and exhausted. Unfortunately, when the Rescue Ship came alongside the boat, one of the occupants made a grab at the scrambling net and capsized the boat, trapping several men underneath and causing them to be drowned. The rest clung to the nets, but the movement on the ship was so great that it seemed impossible to employ the ordinary means of rescue. Nevertheless it was clear that if any were to be saved the utmost speed was necessary. Captain Good saw that the only hope lay in opening the 'cattle doors' abreast the forward well-deck, above the men. It was a risk, but it had to be taken. His crew stood by secured to lifelines and the doors were opened. When the ship rolled towards the men in the water they were lifted up and washed in through the opening. Here they were grabbed by strong hands and

E

prevented from being washed back again. In this way a further ten men were saved by the rescue squads who were themselves often up to their necks in the swirling water which poured through the gap in the bulwarks.

While this rescue work was in progress, reports were received that four more ships had been torpedoed. The *Melrose Abbey* set out to search for survivors. Her speed was five knots, which was all that she could make in the prevailing sea and weather conditions. She found four men clinging to an upturned lifeboat and rescued them. Soon afterwards a second boat was sighted containing one man and four dead companions. Both these boats belonged to the Norwegian ship *Bonnieville* in which the Commodore of the convoy had been embarked. He was lost, together with his staff.

Later, while proceeding to rejoin the convoy, a raft carrying two survivors from the British ship *Nailsea* was sighted. One man was rescued, but the other got his foot jammed in the raft, and the lifeline thrown to him fouled the lifelight on top of his head. Due to the violent movement of the raft, he was dragged to and fro with his head under water, and despite the valiant efforts of the Third Officer to free him he was drowned.

Although further wide sweeps were made, no more survivors from the four ships were found. It took the *Melrose Abbey* twenty-two hours to rejoin the convoy, which she found hove to because of the weather. While engaged on these hazardous operations she secured one hundred and sixty-seven

HF/DF bearings of U-boats, seventy-seven of which were first-class.

A tribute to Captain Good's handling of these rescue operations is contained in a letter written by his Chief Engineer, Mr A. B. Low : ' From 7.30 p.m. till 8 a.m. with mountainous seas running, Captain Good handled his ship in a manner which won the admiration of the entire ship's company. . . . For hours he steamed round, the ship swept at times by huge seas, and when a raft or lifeboat was found, by superb seamanship he brought his ship round to form a lee side, right alongside both lifeboats and rafts. By doing this many lives were saved which otherwise would certainly have been lost. . . . It is one of the wonders of the world when a Master gets praise from a Chief Engineer, but I, like the rest of the crew, feel his deeds should not pass unrecorded.'

Towards the end of April 1943 a welcome addition was made to the Rescue Ship Fleet when another of the Clyde Shipping Company's ships, the S.S. *Goodwin*, completed conversion. She had been built in 1917, was of 1,570 gross tons, and had a speed of 12 knots. During her fitting out, advantage was taken of the experience gained in rescue operations already carried out to bring her thoroughly up-to-date, and to this end she was repeatedly visited by an officer of the staff of the Principal Sea Transport Officer on the Clyde. The result was most satisfactory. The best possible use was made of space. Cabin berths were arranged for forty officers, and berths were provided in the 'tween decks for over a hundred and twenty other survivors. Her forward

well-deck was decked in, and this gave additional
survivor space and made her more seaworthy in bad
weather.   Special consideration was given to fitting
out the hospital and the means of evacuating it
quickly in an emergency, and to storage spaces for
extra food and clothing.

By then the layout of sick bays in Rescue Ships
had become more or less standardised.   As a rule a
bay contained six (sometimes eight) cots, two single
and the rest double-tiered.   A completely fitted bath-
room and a lavatory were sited near by.   When space
allowed, a small separate store and dispensary were
added ; otherwise they were combined with the sick
bay or the operating theatre.   The theatre was originally equipped with a wooden table which had straps
to hold the patient and the surgeon to the table in a
seaway.   These were subsequently replaced by proper
metal surgical tables, fitted with flaps so that plaster
work could be done efficiently.   The British Sailors'
Society made a grant towards the new tables ; but
unfortunately while they were satisfactory for use
ashore, they were much too flimsy to withstand the
violent motion to which the Rescue Ships were
frequently subjected.

During a visit to Halifax by the Rescue Ship *Bury*,
the Medical Officer, Surgeon Lieutenant S. D. Moss,
R.N.V.R., had managed, on his own initiative and
with the help of the Canadian Red Cross Society, to
get his operating table replaced by one of a much
more robust type.   This proved to be in every way
suitable.   As it was not possible to manufacture such
tables in Britain during the war, Surgeon Rear-

Admiral Sir John McNee, Consulting Physician to the Royal Navy in Scotland, who had made the medical equipment of the Rescue Ships his special concern, took up the matter with the British Sailors' Society and the Admiralty Medical Department. As a result, in due course all the ships were equipped with Canadian-type operating tables. Much credit was also due to Mr H. C. Murphy, President of the Nova Scotia Division of the Canadian Red Cross, who obtained the tables and shipped them to Britain.

The equipment of the theatre included a Nuffield anaesthetic apparatus, sterilisers, main and auxiliary (battery) lighting, and a ' double two ' set of surgical instruments, adequate for performing all ordinary major surgery. A small library of medical and surgical books was provided, and an ample supply of Neil-Robertson stretchers, splints, and plaster of Paris. Nothing was spared to perfect the medical and surgical equipment of these ships, and Sir John McNee made it his business to see that the Medical Officers were able to obtain what they needed from the Admiralty, the Red Cross, and the British Sailors' Society.

On her first voyage, which began on 28th April 1943, the *Goodwin*'s coal consumption was found to be abnormally high, being almost thirty-six tons a day at moderate speeds. She was therefore diverted to Iceland to replenish her bunkers, and she returned to the Clyde with one of the small convoys plying between there and the United Kingdom. A straggler from the convoy, the S.S. *Rosenberg*, was torpedoed and sank during a heavy gale, and although the *Good-*

win searched the area for a considerable time, only one survivor was found clinging to a raft, and he died later after being rescued.

After a new propeller had been fitted, and some ballast removed and the remainder redistributed, the *Goodwin*'s coal consumption was much improved and anxiety about her ability to cross the Atlantic was removed.

When the Battle of the Atlantic reached its climax in the spring of 1943 there were still only ten Rescue Ships in service. The *Goodwin* had replaced the *Stockport*, the *Zaafaran*'s successor, the *St Sunniva*, had been lost, and there was still no replacement for the *Toward*. However, the *Copeland*, after her adventurous voyage to North Russia and back, had returned to the transatlantic convoys. She was still under the command of that very able Master, Captain W. G. Hartley, D.S.C.

On the night of 16th May 1943 an escort to the west-bound Convoy ONS7, the British ship *Aymeric*, was torpedoed, and the *Copeland* at once went to her assistance. While she was approaching, a second torpedo struck the *Aymeric*, showing that the U-boat was still in the vicinity. Not only did Captain Hartley have to contend with this hazard, but one of the rear ships in the convoy opened fire in his direction; fortunately the shots fell short. There was a moderate north-westerly gale blowing, and when Captain Hartley reached the scene he found the survivors of the *Aymeric* widely scattered. Some were on rafts, some in water-logged boats; but from the number of red lights showing he could see that the majority of them were in the sea. As the temperature of the sea was only 36°F the crew of the *Copeland* set to with a will to save the men, jumping on to the rafts as they came alongside and bending on lines to haul the survivors on board. The Boatswain, Mr William Moffat, was indefatigable in his efforts, springing on to the rafts and going down the scrambling net until he was waist deep in the icy water to pull men out of the sea. But despite their valiant efforts, out of a crew of seventy-seven only twenty-five were saved. Seven of these were picked up by the trawler *Northern Wave*, which was screening the *Copeland* during the operation. The trawler had recovered fourteen survivors, but seven of them died before they could be transferred to the Rescue Ship.

The ill effect of the shortage of Rescue Ships was brought home by the following series of events. After the rough handling which the *Zamalek* had received with the Arctic convoys, she had to undergo a major refit. She returned to service in December 1942, with Captain Morris still in command and with most of her original crew, and sailed at the end of the month as part of the escort of the outward-bound Convoy ON151. The inevitable winter gales were met on passage and she was obliged to put into St John's, Newfoundland, for fuel. Between that port and Halifax heavy snowstorms and dense fog prevailed, and she reached the end of her voyage with several feet of ice coating her deck and bridge.

The *Zamalek* was destined to take part in what has been described as ' one of the biggest convoy

battles of the whole war '.* At the end of February
1943 the enemy established two patrol lines, comprising some thirty-four U-boats (later reinforced by
a further six) across the expected routes of the transatlantic convoys, in an area which at that time was
outside the range of air cover. This he was able to
do with a fair degree of accuracy by virtue of information received from his radio-intelligence organisation.
The first convoy to cross the patrol lines after they
were established was the east-bound SC121. It was
not sighted, but it lost thirteen ships, nearly all
stragglers, to U-boats ordered to chase after it when
it was discovered that it had eluded the trap. There
was no Rescue Ship with the convoy to pick up
survivors, and fifty who had been rescued by the
destroyer H.M.S. *Harvester* were lost when this war-
ship became a victim of torpedo attack.

The *Zamalek* was attached to the next east-bound
convoy, SC122, and sailed from Halifax on 8th
March. The convoy consisted of fifty-two ships.
On 15th March, when it had reached the dangerous
area beyond the reach of air cover, a gale of hurricane
force sprang up. This later moderated and turned
to heavy snowstorms. The U-boats on patrol made
contact with the convoy during the morning of the
16th, but the first attack did not take place until
eight minutes past midnight of the 17th. Four ships
were torpedoed in quick succession. The *Zamalek*
was on the scene twenty minutes later, but no boats
were found, although many men were seen bobbing
about in the water by the flashing red lights on their

* See *The War at Sea*, Vol. II, p. 365. Roskill

life-jackets. The rescue motorboat was launched, and for the next four hours it cruised around picking up load after load of survivors and ferrying them back to the Rescue Ship. Meanwhile the *Zamalek* was searching the area and picking up survivors from rafts and wreckage. She was within two cables of one of the torpedoed ships when it broke in two with a loud explosion and sank. The rescue operation took six and a half hours, and when a count was made it was found that one hundred and thirty-four survivors had been picked up, of whom three were found to be dead. The numbers were made up as follows : S.S. *Kingsbury*, forty-four ; S.S. *Fort Cedar Lake*, fifty ; S.S. *King Gruffyd*, twenty-five ; and S.S. *Aldermin*, a Dutch ship, twelve. When the *Zamalek*, in company with one of the escorts, was regaining her station in the convoy, a U-boat was heard transmitting close by. Captain Morris took evasive action and safely rejoined the convoy. During his absence two more ships had been torpedoed, but escorts had picked up the survivors.

The attacks continued all day, but it was not until the evening of the 17th that another ship, the Greek S.S. *Carras*, was torpedoed. No distress rockets were fired and no radio message was received, and Captain Morris had some difficulty in finding her, especially as heavy rain squalls were prevalent at the time. At length he came across her lifeboats, from which thirty-four survivors were picked up.

With one hundred and sixty-five survivors then on board, Captain Morris asked permission to proceed independently to the Clyde. This was granted and

E 2

an escort was detailed to screen his ship. All the survivors were landed at Gourock on 22nd March. A glowing tribute was paid to the *Zamalek* by one of the survivors, the Master of the S.S. *Kingsbury*, Captain W. Laidler. In a letter to her owners he said : ' On behalf of the officers, ratings and myself, I beg to place on record our appreciation and deep gratitude to Captain Morris, all officers, Doctor and sick bay staff, stewards and ratings of the *Zamalek* for the wonderful work they carried out in our rescue on 17th March 1943. No praise can be high enough for the undaunted way in which the work of rescue was done in the face of extreme danger, combined with the heavy weather prevailing at the time. The Merchant Service has every reason to be proud of such men, and grateful, for had it not been for the *Zamalek* the loss of life would undoubtedly have been very heavy. The *Zamalek* will always be to me, the little ship with a big heart, and worthy of the gallant men who man her. May they always be blessed with good fortune in their splendid work.'

Coming up behind the *Zamalek*'s convoy and overtaking it was another and faster one, for which again no Rescue Ship was available. Like SC121 the convoy suffered very heavily at the hands of the U-boats, losing thirteen ships. Although the escorts did all they possibly could to rescue survivors, they were engaged with one of the heaviest concentrations of U-boats ever met with in an Atlantic convoy battle, and the loss of life was great.

Before the *Zamalek* set out on her nineteenth voyage, Captain Morris took some well-earned leave, and was replaced by Captain W. H. Hatcher. When five days out, *Zamalek* was instructed to search for a lifeboat which had been sighted by an aircraft in a position about forty miles from the convoy. After a search lasting three and a half hours, the boat was found. It contained seven men from the S.S. *Shillong*, which had been torpedoed and sunk eight days previously. Originally the boat had contained thirty-eight members of the crew, but thirty-one had died from exposure and all the survivors were suffering from immersion feet, frostbite and gangrene.

On the return voyage the *Zamalek* was attached to a convoy and several unsuccessful attacks were made on it. These were repulsed, the enemy losing four U-boats. The Escort Commander was Commander (now Admiral Sir Peter) Gretton. 'It was a great thing,' he wrote, 'to have a Rescue Ship with the convoy again, there never being enough of these invaluable ships to go round. . . . In fact with their wide experience of convoy work, they were almost as good as an extra escort, although they had no means of offence.' *

No series of incidents in the long and hard-fought battle against the U-boats underlined more effectively than did those just described how great was the need for Rescue Ships with every convoy. The U.S. naval historian, Rear-Admiral S. E. Morison, has written of this period : 'The enemy never came so near to disrupting communications between the New World

---

* *Convoy Escort Commander*. Vice-Admiral Sir Peter Gretton, K.C.B., D.S.O., O.B.E., D.S.C. Cassell, 1964. p. 153

and the Old as in the first twenty days of March 1943. Clearly we could not go on losing ships and men at that rate. When convoy after convoy came in with six to a dozen ships missing, the morale of the seamen who had to make the next voyage was impaired. The patriotism, the energy and the sheer guts that kept these men of the Merchant Service, and of the three escorting navies, to their allotted task, is beyond all praise.'*

* *The United States Navy in World War II.* Rear-Admiral S. E. Morison

8

Gadflies

In the official history of the Merchant Navy, 1939-
44, the Master of a Rescue Ship is quoted as saying :
' We don't look much more than a gadfly on the
water, you know. We're not only Rescue Ship, but
we're errand boy and charlady and God knows
what.' * His comment was fully justified. So handy
and efficient were these little ships that whenever a
new requirement arose in the convoy organisation
the first question asked was, ' Can the Rescue Ship
do it ? ' Thus when the Merchant Ship Aircraft
Carriers, known as the ' MAC Ships ', and Escort
Carriers became available to give the convoys air
cover in areas beyond the reach of shore-based aircraft, it was the Rescue Ships which were told
to act as ' Crash Ships ' during flying operations.
This meant they had to follow in the wake of a
carrier and be prepared to rescue any aircraft crew
which had to land in the sea. This duty they performed with their customary efficiency, rescuing in
all thirty-two airmen, only one being lost when he
was carried down by his sinking aircraft. On one
occasion three men were picked up within four
minutes of a crash.

* *British Merchantmen at War.* J. L. Hodson. H.M.S.O., p. 45

The normal station for a Rescue Ship was at the rear of one of the middle columns of a convoy. They were thus in a good position for passing and repeating signals, a circumstance made much use of by Commodores of Convoy. Most important of all, however, was the fact that on board was a doctor and first-class medical equipment, available throughout the voyage for dealing with sick and injured. There might be from three to five thousand officers and men sailing in company, and there were plenty of opportunities for saving life and tending injured men besides those resulting from enemy action. All the same, it was not quite so easy to 'send for the doctor' as it sounds, especially in stormy weather, perhaps with darkness approaching or with indications that a U-boat attack was about to develop. To enable a proper assessment to be made of the risks, it was desirable that more information should be conveyed to the Medical Officer on board the Rescue Ship than, for example, a laconic signal from the Commodore: 'Pennant Number 99 has a man requiring urgent medical attention.' Was it a really urgent case, or could it wait until the sea moderated, or until daylight? Clearly the Master of a ship could not be expected to answer such questions as these, dependent as they were on a correct diagnosis of the patient's state. On the other hand a lengthy exchange of signals between the Rescue Ship and that of the patient to enable the Medical Officer to decide on the right course of action was equally undesirable, especially at night, when signals could be made only on a shaded, directional blue light of

limited range. The use of radio was of course out
of the question. It must also be remembered that
ships of many nationalities were sailing in the convoys, and not all the Masters could express themselves clearly in English.

On 10th November 1943, in a letter to the Medical
Director-General of the Navy, Surgeon Rear-Admiral
Sir John McNee stated : ' In a recent convoy passage the Medical Officer of the Rescue Ship *Goodwin*
reports that nearly seventy signals were passed con-
nected with medical aid. Copies of all these signals
have been seen by me, and it is clear that an abbreviated medical code of the type suggested would have
saved much time and some unnecessary boarding of
ships in bad weather.' Sir John had in fact forwarded such a code to the Admiralty through the
Flag Officer-in-Charge, Glasgow, in the previous
July. This was being circulated to the interested
departments in the Admiralty ; it also had to be
agreed with the United States Convoy and Routeing
Authority. Unfortunately all this took time, but
Sir John kept up the pressure and eventually had
the satisfaction of seeing the code issued for use in
March 1944.

The prinipal features of the code were a combination of Alphabetical and Numeral flags preceded
by the Flag W. It conveyed briefly but accurately
to the Medical Officer the essential details of the
case—*e.g.*, injury, illness, part of body involved, thus
enabling him to decide whether an immediate
attempt to visit the sick or injured man was necessary
to save his life or whether boarding might safely be

delayed. The whole code was short enough to be printed on a card which could be hung up in the Communications Centre in every ship. It is reproduced in Appendix III. This simplified medical code proved a great success, and it eased considerably the strain on the hard-worked Medical Officers of the Rescue Ships.

The transfer of a sick or injured man from his own ship to the Rescue Ship in a seaway was often a difficult and tricky evolution. When the S.S. *Aboyne* (1,020 tons, 13 knots) of the Dundee, Perth and London Shipping Company began her service as a Rescue Ship in June 1943, her Master, Captain J. Harris, O.B.E., decided that some better system than the usual transfer by motorboat could be evolved. The idea came to him after watching the operation of a Merryweather turntable ladder supplied to the Fire Services. He conceived the notion of using in a similar manner the forty-foot long forederrick with which his ship was fitted. The Rescue Ship was brought close in on the quarter of the ship from or to which the transfer was to be made. Both ships reduced speed until they just had steerage way, and a rifle rocket to which thirty fathoms of point line had been attached was fired across. To the end of the point line thirty fathoms of two-inch rope were attached, and this in turn was made fast to a hook on the end of the derrick purchase. A similar two-inch line from the hook was manned in the *Aboyne*. If the doctor was required to board, he climbed into a basket and in this was hoisted up and hauled across to the poop of the ship needing him.

' I used to die a thousand deaths every time I climbed into that damned basket, wondering if I would ever get safely across to the other ship,' the *Aboyne*'s Medical Officer, Dr G. M. Baird, wrote recently in a letter to the authors, ' but I had complete confidence in Captain Harris, and we never had an accident.' If a patient had to be transferred, a special kind of canvas stretcher, designed by the Chief Officer, Mr W. Hughes, was used. When all was ready, the patient in the stretcher was lifted to the rail, and, taking advantage of a moment when one ship lifted to the swell as the other dipped, the purchase was hove in and the human freight eased over, the Rescue Ship sheering out as soon as the stretcher was airborne. The derrick was then swung inboard and the patient was landed on deck.

After experience gained during her second voyage (which was the first time the derrick was needed), various improvements were made. The derrick was lengthened to sixty-one feet, thus allowing more room for manœuvre, and improvements were made to the standard line-throwing rifle which greatly increased its range and accuracy. The great advantage of the ' *Aboyne* Method ' was the saving of time. From the moment of firing the line until the patient arrived in the ship's hospital, often no more than four or five minutes elapsed, compared with the minimum of a quarter of an hour taken when using the rescue motorboat. Moreover, in the case of patients with fractured limbs, transfers from ship to ship were made without any of the shocks which inevitably attended a transfer by boat. For the

success of the scheme Captain Harris deserves much
credit.   He was a Scot with an outstanding record.
At sea as an apprentice during the First World War,
he decided that life was not exciting enough, so he
enlisted in the King's Royal Rifle Corps.   Drafted
to France, he was wounded at the Battle of Loos.
After the war he returned to sea, where he earned a
reputation for fearlessness and determination, being
always willing to take risks if the occasion demanded.
With these great qualities went a love of music, and
in the *Aboyne*, whenever weather and other conditions allowed, he would broadcast to ships in company a concert from the radio-gramophone in his
cabin under the bridge.   On one occasion, when a
young Scot on board one of the ships in the convoy
had been killed in an accident, the body was transferred to the *Aboyne* for burial at sea.   Captain Harris
read the Burial Service, and as the body was com-
mitted to the deep he broadcast that wonderful
lament, *The Flowers of the Forest*.   The skirl of the
pipes echoed across the waters of the for once calm
Atlantic, and the dead man'sshi pmates lining the
guard-rails of their own ship were singularly touched
by this thoughtful tribute.

During the two years in which the *Aboyne* was
employed on rescue duty, over sixty cases were
transferred by the method mentioned above, and
innumerable visits were made by the doctor to other
ships, without a single mishap.   Captain Harris's
services were recognised by the award of his O.B.E.
Chief Officer Hughes's keenness and interest in rescue
operations earned him a well-deserved M.B.E.   He

devised a small raft which was fitted with two cock-pits. A member of the Rescue Ship's crew secured himself in one cockpit and the raft was then lowered into the sea close to a survivor. Once the survivor had been hauled into the raft, a line was secured round him, and using this he could be hoisted aboard the Rescue Ship. This method was also adopted by the other ships in preference to the basket slung on the end of a derrick, which was very liable to tip up at a critical moment.

By the time the *Aboyne* began her rescue service, the peak of the Battle of the Atlantic was almost past, hence she did not take part in dramatic rescue opera-tions such as those described in earlier chapters. In fact in the whole of her two years' service she only rescued twenty survivors. But, as has been related, her contribution to the efficiency of the rescue work was great, and the medical attention she was able to provide was equally valuable.

Six of the twenty survivors were airmen. On *Aboyne*'s fourth voyage the crew of three from a Swordfish aircraft belonging to the MAC Ship *Empire McColl* were rescued, and ten cases from the ships in convoy received medical attention. On her next voyage, three Dutch airmen from the MAC Ship *MacGadila* were rescued, thanks to the alertness of the *Aboyne*'s officer of the watch. The weather was thick and the *Aboyne*, acting as ' Crash ' Ship, was following on the quarter of the carrier, which was only just visible. Just before the carrier faded from sight the officer of the watch took a bearing of her. Therefore when, a few moments later, a flash was seen and the noise of an aircraft hitting the water was heard, *Aboyne* was able to run down the bearing and find the three men in the water. They were spotted in the fog by the flashing red lights on their life-jackets. Soon afterwards, acting on a signal from the Senior Officer of the escort force, two corvettes appeared to hunt for the crew of the missing aircraft. Captain Harris was able to inform them that the men had already been recovered and were safe and sound on board his ship.

On *Aboyne*'s tenth voyage another ten cases were transferred by derrick; one, a man with a compound fracture of the leg, taking only four minutes. A suspected case of smallpox taken on board sent the *Aboyne* hurrying over to the Commodore's ship to procure sufficient vaccine to vaccinate both her own crew and that of the ship from which the suspect had come. The man was subsequently found only to have chicken-pox.

That the services of the *Aboyne* were appreciated is shown by the signal made to her by Commodore Sir Arthur Baxter, R.N.R: 'Rescue Ship *Aboyne*, Captain Harris, Master, displayed great skill in transferring sick and injured from merchant ships by derrick in all weathers—always keen and alert—deserving of great praise.'

In the summer, fog and icebergs are an ever-present menace to shipping off the Grand Banks of Newfoundland. On 18th June 1943 the Rescue Ship *Gothland*, Master Captain J. M. Haddon, O.B.E., had the misfortune to collide with an iceberg while steaming at 9 knots in thick weather. Although her stem and forecastle were pushed back several feet, the ship was not holed below the waterline and no one was injured. She returned to Halifax, where repairs requiring several weeks were carried out.

Two months later, on 18th August, the Rescue Ship *Bury*, still commanded by her redoubtable Master, Captain L. E. Brown, O.B.E., was escorting a homeward-bound convoy and, in the same area, ran into dense fog. At nine-forty p.m. the lookouts on her bridge observed a large red glow astern, and this was followed by the noise of exploding ammunition. The visibility was about twenty yards, and although no radio message had been received to indicate what had occurred Captain Brown decided to investigate. Because of the fog the convoy had become somewhat disorganised, so he could not be sure where the other ships were or how near they were, but he took the risk of turning round and had several narrow escapes from collision with ships coming towards him. Then the fog lifted a little, and he sighted ahead a vessel alight from stem to stern and surrounded by burning oil. He began to search the area for survivors, and while he was doing so he sighted another vessel, also on fire, but the fog closed down again and it was lost to view.

A burning lifeboat was found. From it three men were rescued—just in time, for they were badly burned about their faces, arms and hands. They were rushed below to the hospital for treatment. Soon afterwards two more men were picked up from a raft, which was also on fire. In the stillness of fog sound travels in a remarkable way, and suddenly all

on the *Bury*'s bridge were electrified by the sound
of powerful motors running at high speed. Correctly
surmising that this might emanate from a U-boat,
Captain Brown ordered everything to be shut down
in case an attack should develop. Soon afterwards one
of the escort vessels reported the presence of a submarine only about two hundred yards from the first
blazing ship, but she must have dived as she was not
seen again and no attack materialised. The *Bury*
continued her search for survivors with the aid of
her searchlights, but without success. The Medical
Officer reported that three of the survivors were in
a very serious condition, so Captain Brown obtained
permission to proceed to St John's, Newfoundland,
to disembark them. On his arrival there, he was
astonished to learn from other survivors, brought in
by escort vessels, that four boatloads of them had
seen his searchlights, but they kept away because
they thought they were those of a U-boat. In consequence they spent two days and nights in their open
boats unnecessarily ; they had not realised that a
U-boat was unlikely to betray her position in such
a way.

One of the most important convoy routes after the
Allied landing in North Africa had taken place was
that between Britain and Gibraltar. Although routed
well away from the enemy-occupied coast of France,
it was not possible for convoys to avoid coming within
range of enemy aircraft based in that country. And
when crossing the Bay of Biscay, the convoy route
took them across the tracks of the U-boats entering
and leaving the Biscay ports. It was while escorting

one of these convoys, designated KMS23, that the gallant Rescue Ship *Rathlin*, then commanded by Captain G. N. Glass, added to the laurels she had already gained during her exploits with the Arctic convoys. During the forenoon of 15th August 1943, six days after leaving the Clyde, a series of air attacks by Focke-Wulf aircraft took place, but no hits were scored. Then, after a pause of six hours, the enemy decided to make a more determined attempt. About twenty aircraft took part in a series of attacks which began at six-five p.m. ' From this time on ' wrote Captain Glass, ' continuous runs were made over the convoy by individual planes, all at very considerable altitude. . . . Bombs were dropped at frequent intervals throughout the convoy, one stick landing between *Rathlin* and her next abeam to starboard, very close to the other ship.' Then at seven p.m. the British ship *Warfield* was hit and started to settle. The *Rathlin* succeeded in rescuing all but one of her crew of ninety-six ; the missing man was believed to have been killed by the explosion of the bomb.

Within five minutes of setting out to rejoin the convoy, the *Rathlin* was singled out for attack by high-level bombers. A stick of bombs which landed only a hundred feet on her starboard bow severely shook the ship. Five minutes later a Focke-Wulf aircraft at a height of about one hundred feet passed down the starboard side a mile away, but despite intense fire from the *Rathlin* and her escorting corvette it survived.

In his report of the incident, the Master specially commended Second Officer R. McRae, who was in charge of the ship's armament of a 12-pdr. gun, a Bofors, and two Oerlikons. McRae also did duty as Navigation Officer, and he managed to fulfil both roles by snatching sun sights between the attacks.

On her next voyage the *Rathlin* was assigned to a transatlantic convoy. In fact two convoys were involved in the battle which was to take place : a slow one, designated ONS18, and a fast one, to which the *Rathlin* was attached, ON202. The fast convoy had sailed after the slow one, and was overhauling it when it became clear to the Admiralty that a U-boat attack was developing on one or both. To pool their defensive resources, they were ordered to combine and form one convoy. They were only about thirty miles apart when the first attack took place. This was on ON202, at five-forty-one a.m. on 20th September 1943. On the bridge of the *Rathlin* two simultaneous explosions were heard ; they appeared to come from the direction of her port bow. It was then noticed that two ships on that bearing were in difficulties. As he approached them, Captain Glass observed only the bow section of one ship, the American *Theodore Dwight Weld*, remaining afloat. She had been blown in half and the stern portion had sunk almost immediately. The other ship, also an American, the *Frederick Douglas*, had a large hole amidships, but did not appear to be in any immediate danger of sinking. The *Rathlin* therefore concentrated on rescuing the men in the water, which was covered with oil fuel. The rescue motorboat was launched in record time and twelve men from the *Theodore D. Weld* were recovered, while the Rescue

Ship trawled up another twenty-six survivors, most of them in pretty poor shape, having swallowed some of the heavy black oil. This oil was so thick that it choked the circulating system of the motorboat's engine and brought it to a halt. The ship's engineers rapidly stripped it down and had it back in action within half an hour. The oil slick spread for about three miles, and Captain Glass combed it for further survivors. Finding none, he steamed over to the *Frederick Douglas.* This ship was manned by coloured officers and men, and she had managed to launch her own lifeboats without any apparent difficulty. The entire crew of seventy were rescued, including a negress stowaway and the ship's dog.

The *Rathlin* then returned to have a final look at the bow section of the *Theodore D. Weld*, which now appeared to be sinking. It was as well that she did so, because there was one man still on board, and he was taken off by the rescue boat. Among the one hundred and eight survivors in the *Rathlin* there were a number of badly injured, and the ship's Medical Officer, Surgeon Lieutenant W. D. Broughton, R.N.V.R., had to perform five major operations. Only one of the survivors, a lascar, died; he was buried at sea.

Unfortunately the radio message ordering the two convoys to join forces was received in a mutilated condition by the Senior Officer of the escort force with ON202, so it was not until late on the evening of 20th September that the rendezvous with ONS18 took place. That night three attacks were made on the combined convoy. All were repulsed by the

strong and reinforced escort force, but two of the
warships fell victims to a new weapon which the
enemy used on this occasion for the first time, the
acoustic torpedo. The following day dense fog was
encountered, but the U-boats managed to trail the
convoy and shadow it during the night of the 21st-
22nd. They were prevented from attacking by the
fourteen ships of the escort force, although this force
lost yet another of its number. She had on board
the survivors from the two escort ships which had
been lost earlier, and out of the three ships' com-
panies there were only three survivors.

Meanwhile the *Rathlin* had lost touch with the
convoy, which had become scattered because of the
fog, and she found herself alone. Twice she sighted
U-boats, once on the surface and once at periscope
depth, but she took successful avoiding action. She
rejoined the convoy just as the third escort vessel was
torpedoed. The *Rathlin* went to her assistance, but
another escort vessel arrived first on the scene. As
has already been stated, the number of survivors
was pitifully small.

At four forty-eight a.m. on 23rd September the
S.S. *Steel Voyager* was torpedoed, and the crew
abandoned ship and were picked up by the *Rathlin*.
As it was evident that the *Steel Voyager* was in no
danger of sinking, they were ordered by one of the
escorts to return. They did so, and the ship eventually made port. Fog in varying degrees of density
was encountered during the rest of the voyage, and
the *Rathlin* berthed in Halifax just before midnight
on 28th September. ' Throughout the exciting

events of this voyage, I was most deeply impressed
by the magnificent behaviour of my entire crew,'
wrote Captain Glass in his report.

As a result of constant pressure from the Admir-
alty, and a careful scrutiny of the employment of all
ships which might possibly be converted to Rescue
Ships, five more vessels were selected. These came
into service during 1943. They were the Dundee,
Perth and London Shipping Company's vessel
Dundee (1,541 gross registered tons, 12½ knots), in
August; the Clyde Shipping Company's ships
Fastnet (1,415 gross registered tons, 11 knots), in
October, and *Eddystone* (1,550 tons, 12 knots),
in November; the Prince Line's vessel *Syrian
Prince* (1,989 gross registered tons, 12 knots), also
in November; and the General Steam Navigation
Company's ship *Pinto* (1,346 gross registered tons,
12 knots), in December. Thus by the end of the
year the strength of the Rescue Fleet had risen to
seventeen ships. Had it not been for the six lost,
the total would have been closer to the thirty which
was the target at which the Admiralty was consist-
ently aiming.

The best of the new additions was the *Syrian
Prince*. She was larger than any of the others. The
Fastnet, by contrast, was rather too small, and certainly too slow, yet her hospital was larger than the
hospitals in most of the Rescue Ships; it could
accommodate eight patients at a time. The *Pinto*
was a diesel-driven ship, and although this relieved
her Master of the anxiety about bunkers which
plagued most of the coal burners, she was not quite

as reliable. However, she never missed a voyage. Of the five Rescue Ships, only the *Pinto* and the *Dundee* were to be called upon to rescue the crews of torpedoed ships and alas, as will be related later, the *Pinto* herself became a victim of attack.

For the other ships there was no lack of work to be done : monitoring the U-boats' transmissions on HF/DF, rescuing airmen who had come down in the sea, and providing a first-class medical service to the floating population of the convoys which was increasingly appreciated. Writing to Sir John McNee on 1st March 1944, the Commander-in-Chief Western Approaches, Admiral Sir Max Horton, said : ' There is no doubt in my mind that the introduction and work of Rescue Ships during phases of the Battle of the Atlantic when the U-boats were on the offensive did a tremendous lot towards maintaining the high morale of the Merchant Navy at that time. Since last spring, when the U-boats ceased to take a big toll of our convoys, they have been invaluable in attending to the numerous cases of sickness that arise during passage, and also in assisting to detect the enemy before he becomes a danger to the safety of the convoy.'

9

An Efficient Team

SPEAKING in the House of Commons on 7th March 1944 about the falling proportion of ships being lost in the North Atlantic and United Kingdom coastal convoys, the First Lord of the Admiralty Mr A. V. (later Viscount) Alexander said : " In 1941 one ship was lost out of every one hundred and eighty-one which sailed ; in 1942, one out of every two hundred and thirty-three ; in 1943, one out of every three hundred and forty-four. . . . The reduction in the loss of tonnage has been happily reflected in the Merchant Navy casualties, and in 1943, I am glad to say, the number of officers and men lost was roughly only half that in 1942. The Admiralty, in consultation with the Ministry of War Transport, has been able to increase substantially the number of special Rescue Ships which are sailed with the convoys for the sole purpose of rescuing survivors and giving medical attention. Each carries a naval doctor and they are now an integral part of the convoy system. There have been many reports from the naval escorts praising the high standard of seamanship and efficiency of the Masters, officers and crews of these vessels, which have been operated with magnificent courage and efficiency." *

* *Hansard*, Vol. 397, cols. 1897-1900

In claiming that the losses of Merchant Navy personnel had been roughly halved in 1943, the First Lord was referring to those suffered in the North Atlantic and home waters only, because the total figure for all areas, 7,425, was 2,000 higher than in 1942, and only 1,423 less than the peak figure of 8,848 in 1941. The increase in the total number of casualties suffered was due to the large number of sinkings still occurring in other areas, for which no Rescue Ships were available. Whereas the number of ships sunk in the North Atlantic had fallen from 1,006 in 1942 to 284 in 1943, the comparable figures for the Mediterranean were 73 and 137 respectively, and the ships lost outside the North Atlantic in 1943, a total of 313, was greater than that within it.

In 1944 the prospects of further additions to the Rescue Ship Fleet appeared poor. The Ministry of War Transport said that the bottom of the barrel really had been scraped. The *St Clair* had been taken in hand for conversion in November 1943, but would not be ready for sea until June 1944. Beyond that they could hold out no hope of finding any more suitable ships.

During the winter of 1943-44 there was the usual series of gales in the North Atlantic, and in January the sixteen-year-old Rescue Ship *Fastnet*, one of the slowest vessels in the fleet, making her third voyage, was obliged to weather one of the worst of these gales. Her Master, Captain J. McKellar, O.B.E., a valiant Highlander, and certainly one of the most experienced Masters in the Rescue Service, found his seamanship put to a severe test. The convoy he was escorting, ONS27, outward-bound for Halifax, encountered the full force of a westerly gale soon after clearing the Irish coast, and as the wind and sea increased the convoy's speed fell away. So did that of the *Fastnet*, until she was virtually hove to. The wind rose to hurricane force and the little ship, tossed by the mountainous seas, dropped farther and farther astern until the convoy was some hundred miles ahead. Although he knew that even when the weather moderated, with his poor speed it would take him several days to catch up, Captain McKellar decided to carry on. He reasoned that should a ship in the convoy be torpedoed, he could still reach the scene some hours later, possibly in time to save some lives, a factor always in the fore-front of a Rescue Ship Master's mind. His decision was reinforced by the knowledge that there were U-boats in the area. In this way he proceeded, quite alone, three-quarters of the way across the Atlantic. Fortunately no untoward incident took place and his services were not required.

Following close behind the *Fastnet*'s convoy was another westbound one, ON218, escorted by the Rescue Ship *Aboyne*. This too encountered the gale which had severely impeded the progress of ONS27. At four p.m. on 9th January 1944, the *Aboyne* received an urgent signal from an American ship, the *Theodore Parker*, which read : ' We are breaking up. Am preparing to abandon ship. Please stand by.' The weather at the time was not too bad—a fresh south-west wind, with a moderate sea and swell, and the barometer inclined to rise slowly ; but there were indications of a deterioration, and darkness was setting in. The *Theodore Parker* turned and headed eastward, the *Aboyne* following. Then at about seven p.m. the *Theodore Parker* hove to and lowered a boat. Much to Captain Harris's surprise it appeared empty when it drifted past him. Only when he received a message from the American Master asking him if he had recovered the papers and valuables in the boat, did he discover that it contained the ship's papers and $25,000. But by that time it had been lost to sight.

Throughout the night the *Aboyne* and a corvette, H.M.S. *Deveron*, kept company with the damaged vessel, and at seven a.m. the next day the American once again announced her intention of abandoning ship. The *Deveron* steamed up to windward and pumped out oil, which materially calmed the high sea by then running, while the Rescue Ship closed in ready to pick up the crew. Yet when it came to the point the Master of the *Theodore Parker* hesitated to give the order, although assured by Captain Harris that if the men took to their life-rafts he would most certainly pick them up. Eight men did risk it, and all were picked up. From them Captain Harris learned that opinion was divided on the question of the seaworthiness of their ship. It was a difficult decision for her Master to make ; naturally he did not wish to abandon her so long as there was any chance of saving her. The three ships continued in company throughout the day. Then it was the *Aboyne*'s turn for trouble. At two-thirty a.m. on 11th January her steering gear broke down, due in

…ain O. C. Morris, D.S.O.

…ain J. M. Haddon, O.B.E., of the GOTHLAND with Surgeon Lieutenant J. Mackenzie, R.N.V.R.

Captain A. Banning, D.S.O.

Rescue Ship at sea with a convoy

part to the heavy pounding the ship had taken while standing by the *Theodore Parker*. The buffer springs by which the tiller was attached to the quadrant had carried away, freeing the rudder head and tiller, which started to lash about in an alarming manner. The ship, out of control, wallowed in the heavy Atlantic swell and rolled violently. It was with very great difficulty that a chain and wire lashing was passed round the tiller and secured to the quadrant, wedging it tight, with the rudder a few degrees to starboard of the amidships position. In this condition the *Aboyne* managed to make good a course between south-south-east and south. In the evening the wind moderated, and as a result she bore up three to four points, but luckily this still took her in the general direction of the Azores. By the next morning the weather had improved still more. The *Deveron* took the *Aboyne* in tow, and this made possible an attempt to effect a temporary repair to the steering gear. This was difficult, but thanks to the patience, perseverance and ingenuity of the Second Engineer it was eventually accomplished, and the speed of 2 knots was increased to 10. The rudder had been given ten degrees of movement on either side of the centre line. During a squall the tow parted. Despite the restricted movement of his rudder, Captain Harris decided that he could make Horta in the Azores under his own steam. He reached it during the afternoon of 15th January. There he found the *Theodore Parker*; she had made port twenty-four hours earlier.

A less fortunate ship was the United States *Joel*

F

R. Poinsett. She formed part of a west-bound convoy, ON225. The escort included the Rescue Ship *Eddystone*, and that fine seaman Captain A. Banning, D.S.O., had been appointed to her command when she finished her conversion in November 1943. The Chief Officer was Mr (now Captain) A. H. Shearer, a deep-sea Master, and it proved a very successful combination of talents. The convoy became scattered in bad weather, and after regrouping to the south-east of the Grand Banks it encountered a blizzard which coated all the ships with ice. Next a signal was received by the Commodore from the *Joel R. Poinsett* to say that she was breaking in half. She had dropped some ninety miles astern of the convoy, so the *Eddystone* and an escort vessel were detached to look for her. ' I remember it was a full moon and I had most of the men out nearly all night breaking up all the ice we could on the fore-deck,' wrote the Chief Officer in a letter to the authors. With the aid of radar, the wreck was located at daybreak the next day. She presented a curious sight. The fore part of the ship had disappeared, the break having occurred just forward of the bridge. It looked as though it had been cut off with a knife. The after part, on which officers and crew had gathered, was floating on an even keel, though rolling heavily in the swell.

As the *Joel R. Poinsett*'s four lifeboats were intact, Captain Banning decided that it would be better to use these than to use his one motorboat. He signalled accordingly, and was thus able to employ his entire crew in helping the survivors over the side of the

Eddystone. The two boats which were lowered on
the lee side of the drifting hulk had some trouble in
clearing the stern, but those on the weather side got
away without difficulty. The last to leave were the
Captain and the Boatswain. After lowering the last
boat they dived into the icy sea and were picked up
by its crew.

The intense cold made the handling of ropes and
gear a painful process and hampered operations to
such an extent that the afternoon watch was almost
over before the transfer was completed. The total
number saved was sixty-one, and the *Eddystone* subsequently received the thanks of the United States
War Shipping Administration for her work. The
after part of the *Joel R. Poinsett* was eventually
salved and towed into port.

Although on 22nd March 1944 the German Naval
Command virtually conceded victory to the Allies
in the great Battle of the Atlantic, and withdrew its
U-boats from the central part of the ocean, it still
kept a few on patrol, obviously hoping that the
general withdrawal would not become known and so
enable us to transfer forces to other areas.

Convoy SC156 left Halifax early in April 1944.
Included in the escort force was the Rescue Ship
Goodwin, the Master being Captain W. Hartley,
D.S.C., who had distinguished himself in command
of the *Copeland* with PQ18. This convoy was un-
lucky enough to encounter U-302. At two-thirty
a.m. on 6th April she torpedoed the Norwegian motor
ship *South America*, which at once burst into flames
masthead high. The *Goodwin* immediately went to

her assistance. Captain Hartley decided that the only way to save the crew would be to go alongside aft on the windward side, for it looked as if the fire might prevent the crew from manning their boats. The Rescue Ship was about seventy yards astern of the burning vessel when this was struck by another torpedo. This had the unusual effect of quenching the fire. The crew were thus enabled to launch two lifeboats and a raft, and in these all forty-two of them were accommodated. When the second torpedo struck, Captain Hartley had put his helm hard over and gone astern; in consequence the *Goodwin* stopped about forty feet short of the *South America* and swung across her stern at right angles, with her bridge in line with it. She was thus in an ideal position to rescue the survivors. From the time of the first attack until the last man clambered over the Rescue Ship's side, only thirty-seven minutes elapsed. The owners of the *South America*, the Texas Oil Company, in a letter of appreciation forwarded to the Ministry of War Transport by the War Shipping Administration, remarked on the excellent work of the officers and men of the *Goodwin* ' in rescuing the entire crew of the *South America* without injury. Her Master, Captain Ambjornsen, while praising the way in which the rescue was effected, also expressed gratitude for the way the survivors were treated on board the *Goodwin*.'

U-302 scored a second success by torpedoing the Norwegian S.S. *Ruth*. The survivors, numbering thirty-six, were picked up by H.M.S. *Chelmer* and later transferred to the *Goodwin*. The U-boat was later sunk by H.M.S. *Swale*.

No further attacks on the convoy took place, but the propeller shaft in the American ship *Oldham* broke and she had to be abandoned. The *Goodwin* took on board the fifty-six members of her crew, bringing the total number of survivors on board to one hundred and thirty-four.

The *Goodwin*'s next two voyages, one to Halifax and the other to Gibraltar and back, were comparatively uneventful. She was then given an unusual assignment at Moville, on Lough Foyle, in Northern Ireland. The German U-boats operating from French ports on the Bay of Biscay, having suffered severely as a result of Coastal Command's Bay offensive and the operations of the United States Navy's hunter-killer groups working off the Azores, had been transferred to Norwegian ports. Also the introduction of the *schnorkel* enabled them to charge their batteries without surfacing, and allowed them once again to begin operations in the coastal waters of the United Kingdom. The Admiralty was concerned for the safety of some large troopships due to pass north of Ireland, and expected that a determined attack on them would be made. It was considered that if one of these ships were to be torpedoed and sunk, the loss of life would be heavy. A Rescue Ship was specially equipped for saving life at sea, and although too slow to keep up with the troopships, if stationed at Moville she could reach the scene of a disaster within a reasonable period of time.

The *Goodwin* was kept at Moville, with steam at five minutes' notice, for twenty-six days, by no means an easy feat for a ship with coal-fired Scotch-type boilers. But her success in accomplishing it was rewarded when on 8th September she was ordered to proceed to rescue the crew of the whale oil tanker S.S. *Empire Heritage*, which had been torpedoed at four a.m. that day off the north coast of Ireland. She was under way within two minutes of receiving the order. But after only ten minutes' steaming she was recalled. In the light of subsequent events, the decision to do so was unfortunate. The *Empire Heritage* had a displacement of 15,000 dead-weight tons. She was hit in the 'tween-deck which ran throughout the length of the ship, and the sea gaining access to such a large space, she quickly capsized and sank. The Rescue Ship *Pinto*, Master Captain L. S. Boggs, M.B.E., a gallant Australian, formed part of the escort of the *Empire Heritage*'s convoy. She was soon on the scene to rescue survivors, who could be seen by the lights on their life-jackets bobbing about in the water. The first two had been picked up, and were being examined by the Medical Officer, Surgeon Lieutenant P. N. Holmes, R.N.V.R., when a periscope was sighted crossing ahead from starboard to port. The *Pinto*, being stopped, was unable to gather way quickly enough to ram the U-boat, and the next instant she herself was struck by a torpedo and sank within a minute. Dr Holmes was on his way to the hospital when the ship was hit. He subsequently wrote the following account of the disaster : ' I had got to a point near the coal locker which lies up against the operating theatre when there was a rushing sound blended into a tremendous explosive crash. The deck seemed to jump up and the whole ship to shudder. Smoke, coal and water were all around. I was flung against the rails and temporarily dazed by quantities of debris, including considerable amounts of galley coal which landed on my head and back. Much of the superstructure of the ship seemed to be crashing down. I tried to locate the sick-berth attendant, and a few seconds later heard his voice from somewhere outside. The ship was already heeling over and beginning to sink by the stern. Water was rushing along the alleyway. I went to make sure that the hospital was clear and then went to report to the Captain. He was standing against the rails opposite the port entrance to his cabin shouting to the men to get over the side. Some were getting into the dinghy which was slung outboard. I next went down the ladder to have another look round, and about three seconds after I had spoken to the Captain the ship seemed to make a sudden drop. I was standing on the deck up to my waist in water when I last saw the Captain. I was carried down a long way, and became jammed against the rigging, possibly one of the stays. When I became free I began to rise again, and on reaching the surface, about half a minute later, the ship had gone.'

Neither Captain Boggs nor the occupants of the dinghy was seen again. Dr Holmes and forty other survivors clung to the wreckage for about two hours before being rescued by H.M. Trawler *Northern Wave*. This ship and escort vessels from the convoy also picked up forty-six survivors from the *Empire*

Heritage. Despite his unnerving experience, as soon as Dr Holmes was on board the trawler he and the sick berth attendants set to work to tend the survivors. The Master, the Chief Engineer, Mr A. W. Thomson, and fourteen members of the *Pinto*'s crew, including seven D.E.M.S. ratings, were lost. This was the seventh, and mercifully the last, of the Rescue Ships to be sunk when carrying out their dangerous and humanitarian work. Altogether two hundred and sixteen officers and men, including five Masters of the Rescue Service, lost their lives in attempting to save others.

The struggle was not yet over. On 18th October 1944 the Rescue Ship *Dundee*, Master Captain J. Murray, O.B.E., escorting the outward-bound Convoy ONC260 encountered the full fury of an Atlantic gale which scattered the merchant ships far and wide. At six-fifty p.m. Captain Murray received a signal from the Senior Officer of the escort to close a ship in distress and rescue her crew. Three of the escort vessels had already attempted to do so, but without success.

The ship in distress was an L.C.T. (Landing Craft, Tank) of about 1,000 tons displacement. Having very little freeboard, she presented a particular problem. When the *Dundee* sighted her she was practically awash and entirely at the mercy of a fifty-mile-an-hour wind and a sea with waves estimated at between twenty and thirty feet high. The *Dundee* closed to windward of the waterlogged craft, but when her Commanding Officer signalled that his ship was making water fast and that he wished to abandon ship, Captain Murray took the *Dundee* round to leeward of her. All attempts to get a line across to the L.C.T. failed. Although there was a considerable risk of over-riding her, Murray could see that the only hope of effecting a speedy rescue was to put his ship alongside. This he did, and four of the twenty men on board the sinking vessel jumped on to the boom net. A fifth managed to leap on to the *Dundee*'s deck before the sea brought the two ships together with such force that one of the men on the boom fell off and was crushed. The *Dundee* was holed, providentially above the water-line, but she had to withdraw to prevent further damage. Another attempt to get a line across was successful, and three more men were hauled to safety on a raft which capsized several times, almost drowning them. Soon afterwards the L.C.T. sank and the twelve remaining men took to a raft. Captain Murray kept his searchlights trained on it as he tried to close it. The seas were so mountainous that several men were washed off before he got alongside it. Then, despite the heroic efforts of the *Dundee*'s crew to save them, several men were crushed against the ship's side and killed. One man gripped the scrambling net so tightly that it was necessary to cut the net away round his hands to release him and haul him on board. One man in a kapok lifebelt was being hauled up the side; it broke just as he reached deck level, and he fell back into the sea and was lost. In all, twelve of the L.C.T.'s crew were saved. One of these died soon afterwards as a result of the injuries he had received, and the remainder were in a

F 2

sorry state, battered, bruised and half-drowned. Captain Murray specially commended the work of the ship's Medical Officer, Surgeon Lieutenant A. W. Smith, R.N.V.R., for his untiring efforts to resuscitate the survivors, and there is no question that many of them owed their lives to his skill and attention. For his service on this occasion he was awarded the O.B.E.

On her return to Liverpool the *Dundee* was visited by the Commander-in-Chief Western Approaches, Admiral Sir Max Horton, and he congratulated the Master and his crew on their fine work in effecting a rescue under such difficult conditions of weather and darkness.

The loss of the *Pinto*, the inability of the Ministry of War Transport to provide any more suitable vessels for conversion, and the fact that corvettes in ever-increasing numbers were being delivered, led the Admiralty to allocate five of these vessels, still on the stocks, for completion as Rescue Ships. Although their speed of 16 to $16\frac{1}{2}$ knots gave them a distinct advantage over the other Rescue Ships in service, they were not an ideal choice. Their short length, large overhanging stern, large bow flare and tumble-home sides did not favour boat work. Internally, it was found impracticable to fit for survivors the bunks to which merchant seamen are accustomed. Instead hammocks were used, the spaces beneath being used as mess decks, as in naval vessels of that period. Fortunately the problem of lashing up and stowing hammocks which these arrangements invited never arose, for by the time the ships came into service the war in Europe was drawing to a close.

In accordance with the Ministry of War Transport policy for naming war-built British ships, all the new-type Rescue Ships carried the prefix ' Empire '. It was decided that each ship should do three short trips so that the officers and men could become accustomed to their new vessel before attempting an Atlantic crossing. The ships therefore accompanied Gibraltar convoys for the first three days of their passage, and then transferred to homeward-bound convoys, making a round trip of about a week.

The first converted corvette, the *Empire Rest*, came into service on 12th November 1944. She was followed on 10th February 1945 by the *Empire Peacemaker*, and on 25th February by the *Empire Comfort*. On 7th March, after an accident which delayed her considerably, the *Empire Lifeguard* became operational. The last ship, the *Empire Shelter*, entered service on 16th April 1945. These ' Empire ' Rescue Ships covered forty convoys, and although (with one exception) they were not called upon to rescue any survivors, they performed satisfactorily all the other duties of Rescue Ships.

Experience with the *Empire Rest* on a transatlantic convoy, when very heavy weather was encountered, revealed that the bunker capacity of these ships would permit of a direct Atlantic crossing only under favourable weather conditions and at the same time leave a sufficient margin of fuel for rescue work. As a result, orders were issued to fit all of them for oiling at sea. But because at the height of the battle Rescue Ships often became detached from their convoys for long periods, a more satisfactory answer would have been to have increased the amount of fuel carried.

The last rescue of the war was made by the *Gothland*, one of the original Rescue Ships. She was commanded throughout her three and a half years' service by the indomitable Captain James Haddon, O.B.E., ably supported by his Chief Engineer, D. McAddie, O.B.E., and, from February 1944, by the Medical Officer, Surgeon Lieutenant T. S. Eimerl, D.S.C., V.R.D., R.N.V.R. It was said of this highly efficient ship that hardly a trip went by when she did not receive some signal from the Commodore or Senior Officer of the escort of the convoy to which she was attached thanking her for her valuable assistance.

On this, the penultimate voyage of her career as a Rescue Ship, she was escorting a transatlantic convoy. On 18th April 1945 she was in her usual station astern of the escort carrier, for which she was acting as ' Crash ' Ship, when an explosion was heard on the starboard side of the convoy. An American ship, the *Cyrus H. McCormick*, was seen to be on fire after having been torpedoed. The *Gothland* proceeded towards her at full speed. It was then noticed that a second ship, the British *Empire Gold*, had also been hit. Within thirteen minutes of hearing the sound of the explosion, the *Gothland*'s rescue motorboat was in the oil-covered water, picking up survivors from the two ships. During the rescue operations a series of violent explosions was taking place on board the *Empire Gold*. These, and the wreckage and the thick oil surrounding the burning ship, made for a highly dangerous situation. However, forty-seven members of the crew of the *Cyrus H. McCormick* were picked up, but only three from the *Empire Gold*. The survivors were covered in black oil, and twenty-four of them required medical attention. The whole rescue operation was completed in an hour and a quarter. After a final search of the area to make sure that no survivor had been overlooked, the *Gothland* rejoined the convoy.

In addition to this rescue, the *Gothland*'s rescue motorboat made four trips to ships in the convoy requiring medical assistance, and medical advice was passed by loud-hailer to twenty-eight other ships. There could be no more eloquent testimony to the invaluable work performed by the Rescue Ships and to the part they played in bringing about victory at sea with which to close this account of their activities.

On the cessation of hostilities in Europe the Admiralty sent the following message to the Rescue Ships and all those concerned in their operation :

The Rescue Ships that supported and succoured our convoys throughout the darkest days of the Battle of the Atlantic are now returning to their normal duties, having saved over four thousand lives.

The steadfast gallantry with which the Masters, Officers, and crews of these ships carried out their duties in the face of great danger has played no small part in our victory at sea, and has won the admiration, gratitude and esteem of the Royal Navy. 291616/May 1945.

The Commander-in-Chief Western Approaches,

Admiral Sir Max Horton, G.C.B., D.S.O., also paid
them a tribute :

On the termination of the Rescue Ship Service, I wish to
express my warmest appreciation of service rendered. Throughout the Battle of the Atlantic, these ships have rendered con-
spicuous service in the most arduous conditions. Their unfailing
spirit of co-operation with H.M. Ships and the high degree of
seamanship displayed, has been a source of admiration to us all.
The Rescue Ships have made a substantial contribution to Victory
in the Atlantic. 291709/May 1945.

The manner in which their services were appreciated by the Commodores of Convoy is summed up
in a message sent by Commodore E. C. Denison,
R.N.R., on 11th April 1944 :

It is desired to pay a tribute to the Rescue Ships attached to
the North Atlantic convoys.

In addition to their invaluable help when a disaster occurs,
their presence in the convoy inspires a great feeling of confidence,
which contributes to a large extent towards keeping up the high
morale of the personnel of the convoys. They are always in
station, however bad the weather may be, and they are of very
great assistance to the Commodore both in repeating signals and
in keeping him informed of what is going on in the rear of the
convoy.

It is considered that the Masters, Officers, and crews, and
Medical Officers and their staffs, of these ships are worthy of the
highest praise and have earned the gratitude of all sailing in
convoys.

Epilogue

TWENTY-ODD rusty, battered, salt-sprayed but gallant little Rescue Ships survived the war. Some of their exploits have been recounted in this book. They steamed an estimated two and a quarter million miles to accompany seven hundred and ninety-seven convoys, including twenty-seven to North Russia. All have found their way to the breaker's yard. Even the doughty *Zamalek*, with a war record as proud as any—sixty-four convoys and six hundred and eleven lives saved (Captain Morris claims six hundred and sixty-five)—met an ignominious end when she was sunk as a blockship in the Suez Canal by order of President Nasser during the operations there in 1956.

Evidence of the high esteem with which the services of the officers and men who manned these ships was regarded is provided by the list of one hundred and twenty-four Awards, Decorations and Mentions in Despatches which they received. These included two awards of the Distinguished Service Order, sixteen appointments as Officers of the British Empire, nine Distinguished Service Crosses, one George Medal, six Distinguished Service Medals, and twenty-four British Empire Medals. In addition, there were twelve recipients of Lloyd's War Medal for Bravery

at Sea. To these must be added the awards made
to the Medical Officers ; these included one appointment as an Officer of the Order of the British Empire,
two Distinguished Service Crosses, one as a Member
of the Order of the British Empire, and two Mentions
in Despatches.

It is inevitable that in the twenty-three years which
have elapsed since the Rescue Service was disbanded,
some of its members, including Captains Banning
and Snowden, should have set sail for ' the undis-
covered country from whose bourn no traveller re-
turns '. Others, like Captains McKellar and Harris,
and Chief Radio Officer Horace Bell, are enjoying
retirement in their native Scotland. Quite a number,
like Captains Brown, Glass, Shearer and Hartley, are
still carrying out duties in the port, shipping and
training organisations of this country. Second Officer
R. McRae, who distinguished himself in the *Rathlin*,
applied for a job as a traveller in Scotch whisky when
his eyesight failed. Being a teetotaller he was promptly
engaged, and he is now the manager of his own
business. Most of the Medical Officers were comparatively young men when the war began, and their
work under the most arduous conditions will live for
ever as an epic of human endeavour. Today they
are pursuing their high calling in practices up and
down the country. The burly Doctor Wilkins,
whose constant cheerfulness in the face of adversity
was an inspiration to all with whom he came into
contact, is now a Fellow of the Royal College of
Surgeons and is in charge of a hospital overseas.
One and all can be proud of the part they played in

pioneering a service for which there was no previous precedent and which owed its origin to the humanitarian instinct for saving life which happily, even when men are out to kill one another, still survives.

At first sight it may seem strange that, confronted with the need to inaugurate a Rescue Service for the victims of the German submarine offensive against merchant shipping, the Admiralty did not fit out a number of Hospital Ships to cruise in the areas where the U-boats were active, ready to pick up survivors. In theory at any rate, provided they carried the markings and behaved as required by The Hague Convention of 1907, they should have been perfectly safe, and this would have been an admirable solution of the problem. Larger ships could have been used. These would not have suffered in the same way as the Rescue Ships from the savage buffetings of the elements, and possibly their facilities would have been better. There were, however, several reasons why Hospital Ships were not used.

In the First World War, Germany had refused to grant immunity from attack to Hospital Ships in the English Channel, parts of the North Sea, and in the Mediterranean, even if their identity had been notified. Similarly, during the Second World War Germany, and later Italy, showed complete disregard for the provisions of the Convention, and by the middle of 1941 no less than thirteen Hospital Ships had been sunk, although all had been clearly marked as such. The British Government therefore had every reason for distrusting the use of Hospital Ships in dealing with casualties on the high seas. In any case, under the regulations a Hospital Ship had to be lighted up at night. This meant that she could not keep close touch with a convoy without giving away its position to any U-boats which might be lying in wait for it. Yet, as we have seen, the speed with which a rescue was effected was more often than not a matter of life or death. So if the rescuing ship was not in company with the victim of attack, her usefulness was very much reduced.

In fact, the arguments against fitting out and employing Hospital Ships for use with the convoys were decisive. Their use was never given serious consideration because from the start of hostilities it was known that the enemy took little stock of international agreements unless it was to his advantage to do so. There was, however, a suggestion that fitting the Rescue Ships with High Frequency Direction Finding equipment with which to locate enemy submarines was perhaps somewhat unethical, having regard to the main purpose for which Rescue Ships were needed. But the ships neither claimed nor received any immunity from attack so the Admiralty was perfectly justified in using them for any purpose they had in mind, provided it did not interfere with their primary task of rescuing the survivors of torpedoed vessels. Rescue Ships became, in fact, part and parcel of the anti-submarine effort required to ensure the safety of that merchant shipping which was vital to the prosecution of the war, and they accepted like any other ship of a convoy and its escort the risk of being sunk.

It would be a tragedy if the experience gained and

the sacrifices made were to be forgotten. Britain still depends on the sea for her existence, and should another conflict occur in which shipping is once again the object of attack, she must be prepared to meet it. Even if nuclear weapons were not employed, the chances are that casualties would be heavier than in the past, for the effectiveness and accuracy of modern torpedoes is much greater than it was twenty-five years ago, and the nuclear-powered submarine of today presents a more serious threat as a commerce destroyer than did the U-boats of the last war. The modern rocket-assisted torpedo can be fired from a range that is outside that of detection by a ship's sonar equipment. It is plainly evident that the need for a Rescue Service would be even greater than it was during the Second World War.

In 1949 a Diplomatic Conference was held in Geneva to consider what amendments were needed to the rules of the existing Maritime Convention of 1907, regarding the treatment of sick and wounded in war, and to the rules dealing with prisoners of war and the protection of civilians. The Conference had to consider a large number of recommendations deriving from the experience of two World Wars, in both of which there had been heavy casualties amongst the personnel of the Merchant Navy. After four months of work, the delegates of the sixty-four countries represented adopted four Conventions, none of which, however, were signed by Great Britain, although she did sign the Final Act of the Conference.

The Second Convention defines the duties of

belligerents *vis-à-vis* ' the shipwrecked, wounded and sick of the nations in conflict, whether they be members of the Armed Forces or not, who are at sea, whether in a surface ship, in a submarine, or in an aircraft flying over the sea '. The crews and passengers of merchant ships are also covered by Article 13 of the Fourth Convention, which relates to the protection of civilians in time of war. But it is Article 18 of the Second Convention which is of particular interest. It reads :

> After each engagement, Parties in conflict shall, without delay, take all possible measures to search for and collect the ship-wrecked, wounded, and sick, to protect them against pillage, and ill treatment, to ensure their adequate care, and to search for the dead, and prevent their being despoiled.

The obligation is specific, but can it be implemented ?

In a Memorandum to the First Lord, Mr Churchill, dated 29th March 1940, the late Admiral Sir Max Horton wrote : ' This ruthless murder on the high seas, by submarine and aircraft, of non-belligerents (men, women and children) has not its equal in the whole history of warfare, and its complete disregard of every international and moral law should arouse the anger of every nation which pretends to believe in the first principle of justice and human rights. Far from this—we find the smaller neutrals, whose very existence depends on the maintenance of these principles of human rights, not only condone the murderers, but are in effect supporting Germany in numerous ways.' It is of course, pointless to frame rules which are going to be ignored when the time comes to apply them or which it is not possible to carry out. For instance, it is unrealistic to expect a submarine, after having torpedoed a vessel, to surface and carry out the provisions of the article quoted above. As with so many of these attempts to humanise the conduct of war, their intention is altogether admirable, but they tend to ignore the practical difficulties in the way of carrying them out.

In both the United States and Canada a Coastguard Service exists, and although these are paramilitary organisations, they provide, in addition to their other work, a search and rescue service for saving life at sea. Writing about the U.S. Coastguard Service in the *United States Naval Institute Proceedings* for August 1965, the Assistant Secretary of the Treasury, Mr J. A. Reed, said : ' Essentially the Coastguard is a humanitarian agency and its peacetime mission is paramount. In time of emergency, it carries out such duties as are assigned to it under the Navy's mobilisation plans. . . . It should be borne in mind that the Coastguard's military responsibility is carried out concurrently with its peacetime functions ; the one does not supersede the other. Peacetime tasks are not suspended in the event of war. They are merely concentrated to serve the best immediate interests of our country. *Search and rescue capability, for example, becomes an even more pressing responsibility in the event of war when loss of life and shipping are to be anticipated.*' (The italics are by the authors of this book.)

Another activity of the United States Coastguard is its Automated Merchant Vessel Report System (AMVER). It depends on the voluntary co-operation of ships at sea, which are invited to provide daily information of their courses, speeds and destinations. This information is fed into a computer, stored and kept continually up-to-date. At any time that rescue or medical attention may be needed, the computer instantly provides information regarding the nearest available ships in either the Atlantic or the Pacific Oceans. In 1966 the passages of more than 110,000 merchant ships were recorded, and the computer was called upon to provide some 2,550 pictures to help resolve problems arising from misfortunes of one kind or another occurring at sea.

In Canada the Coastguard co-ordinates the marine element in the national Air-Sea Rescue organisation, which in itself is under the overall direction of the Air Section of the Canadian Armed Forces.

In Britain, the Coastguard section of the Ministry of Transport is responsible for the co-ordination of rescue work round the coasts of the British Isles. There are one hundred and fifty-five regular Coastguard stations and one hundred and fifty-three auxiliary ones. The Coastguard Service has no ships or aircraft of its own, but applies to the Royal National Life-boat Institution (R.N.L.I.), the Royal Navy, and the Royal Air Force, for help, according to the circumstances of the case. The R.N.L.I., which was founded in 1824 and which prides itself on the fact that, with the exception of a short period between 1854 and 1869, it has maintained itself entirely by voluntary contributions, now finds itself ' in the red ' due to steadily rising costs. Yet there is great reluctance to apply for a Government subsidy, for this would necessarily involve a degree of Ministerial control. But as the *Torrey Canyon* disaster showed, there are times when the co-ordinated effort which an integrated Rescue Service organisation would provide is badly needed. Such a service could form the nucleus of the one which will most certainly be required should shipping once again come under attack. During both World Wars the R.N.L.I. was allowed to continue on a voluntary basis and it performed magnificent work in saving the lives of those victims of war shipwrecked off our coasts. But today, with the decline of the coastal fleet due to rail and road competition, and the increasing use being made of helicopters and other aircraft for rescue work, there appears to be a need to consider a new approach to the problem of saving life at sea off the coasts of the British Isles.

Although it is difficult without full international co-operation to suggest what steps should be taken to implement the proposals drawn up at the Geneva Conventions referred to above, it is as well to bear their existence in mind. Writing in *La Revue Maritime* for March 1967, Dr Henri Linon said : ' Confronted less than twenty years after the adoption of the Conventions with the possible occurrence of a general conflict, nuclear, chemical or biological, the Signatories should at least ensure for them a greater hearing in Public debate.'

It is hoped that besides chronicling the brave deeds of the past, this book will direct attention to the needs of the future for saving life at sea.

Appendix 1

NATIONALITIES OF SURVIVORS

British (including Canadian)	2,296
United States	951
Norwegian	369
Greek	141
Russian	104
Dutch	75
Latvian	40
Yugoslavian	21
Filipino	20
Panamanian	81
Swedish	34
French	56
Czech	2
German (ex U-Boat)	4
Total	4,194

Appendix II

DETAILS OF RESCUE SHIPS, CONVOYS ESCORTED, AND SURVIVORS RESCUED

Name	Gross Tonnage	Speed Knots	Date taken up	Date operational	Convoys escorted	Survivors rescued	Remarks
Homestroom	1,875	12¼	— Dec 40	11 Jan 41	12	86	Found unsuitable and withdrawn from service
Toward	1,571	12	14 Dec 40	24 Jan 41	45	341	Lost with 56 of her crew on 7 Feb 1943
Copeland	1,526	11	20 Dec 40	29 Jan 41	72	433	
Zamalek	1,565	12½	28 Oct 40	26 Feb 41	64	611	
Zaafaran	1,567	12½	25 Nov 40	23 Mar 41	29	220	Lost when with Arctic Convoy PQ17, 5 Jul 1942
Perth	2,258	13	— Mar 41	— May 41	60	455	
Walmer Castle	906	15	— Jun 41	12 Sep 41	1	81	Bombed and sunk, 21 Sep 1941, with loss of 11 crew and 20 survivors
Dewsbury	1,686	12	24 Jul 41	29 Sep 41	44	5	
Rathlin	1,599	12½	26 Jul 41	2 Oct 41	60	634	
Stockport	1,683	13½	8 Jul 41	22 Oct 41	15	413	Sunk on 24 Feb 1943 with loss of 64 crew and 91 survivors
Tjaldur	1,130	—	29 Jul 41	26 Oct 41	2	Nil	Found unsuitable and withdrawn from service
Bury	1,686	11⅛	14 Aug 41	27 Dec 41		239	
Gothland	1,286	14	— Nov 41	5 Feb 42	40	149	
Melrose Abbey	1,908	13½	— Mar 41	11 Feb 42	42	86	
Accrington	1,678	11	4 Mar 42	26 Jul 42	40	138	
St Sunniva	1,368	—	20 Sep 42	7 Dec 42	1	Nil	Lost with all hands, 23 Jan 1943
Goodwin	1,569	11½	— Dec 42	28 Apr 43	32	133	
Aboyne	1,020	13	not known	11 Jun 43	26	20	
Dundee	1,541	12½	18 Apr 43	8 Aug 43	26	11	
Fastnet	1,415	11	14 Jun 43	7 Oct 43	35	35	
Eddystone	1,550	12	not known	6 Nov 43	26	64	
Syrian Prince	1,989	12	— Jul 43	18 Nov 43	22	Nil	
Pinto	1,345	12	9 Jul 43	5 Dec 43	9	Nil	Sunk on 8 Sep 1944 whilst picking up survivors
St Clair	1,636	15	— Nov 43	1 Jul 44	14	Nil	First of converted corvettes
Empire Rest	1,327	16	26 Oct 44	12 Nov 44	12	Nil	
Empire Peacemaker	1,333	16	18 Jan 45	10 Feb 45	8	3	'Downed' airmen rescued from the sea
Empire Comfort	1,233	16	6 Feb 45	25 Feb 45	8	Nil	
Empire Lifeguard	1,533	16	14 Nov 44	7 Mar 45	6	Nil	
Empire Shelter	1,336	16	27 Mar 45	16 Apr 45	6	Nil	

Appendix III

Convoy Medical Code

This table is designed so that merchant ships in convoy which do not carry Medical Officers can communicate by Flags or Flashing, when urgent medical assistance is required, with ships such as Rescue Ships or Escort Vessels which have Medical Officers on board.

Serial	Cause of Complaint	Nature of Complaint	Nature of Complaint	Site of Complaint
1	Injury	—	Bleeding from mouth or lungs	Head
2	Internal injury	Pain	Bleeding from the bowels	Throat and lungs
3	Burn	Fracture	Fever	Chest
4	Illness	Insanity	Sore throat	Abdomen
5	Effects of sun	Toothache	Bleeding from injury	Groin
6	Effects of immersion in sea	Cough	Abscess or local suppuration	Arm(s)
7	Effects of gases	Rash	—	Leg(s)
8	Injury from shelling or blast	Vomiting	Fits	Back (torso)
9	Injury from air attack	Diarrhoea	Unconsciousness or collapse	Buttocks
0	—	Breathlessness	Lacerations	—

Signals from the table always consist of the Flag ' W ' followed by three or four numeral pennants. Thus to signal ' Urgent medical assistance required, injury —fractured arm ', the group would be W1376, made up as follows :

Prefix	W
Cause of Complaint	1
Nature of Complaint	3
Nature of Complaint	7
Site of Complaint	6

Index

A

Adelon, S.S. : 34
Admiralty : 7, 8, 17, 33, 113, 123, 135, 153
Aldermin, S.S. : 117
Aldersdale, R.F.A. : 59, 61, 62
Alexander, Viscount (A. V.) : 137
Alm, Gustav : 43, 44
Angelina, S.S. : 42, 43
Annik, S.S. : 103
Archangel : 53, 60, 75, 79, 80
Archdale, Commander H., R.N. : 67
Atheltemplar, S.S. : 88
Aymeric, S.S. : 114
Azerbaijan, M.V. : 57, 58

B

Baird, Surgeon Lieutenant G. M., R.N.V.R. : 125
Baltallin, S.S. : 26
Banning, Captain A. : 53, 54, 96, 142, 156
Baron Renfrew, S.S. : 19
Batna, S.S. : 36
Baxter, Commodore Sir Arthur, R.N.R. : 128
Beachy, S.S. : 54
Bell, Chief Radio Officer Horace : 85-92, 156
Bellingham, S.S. : 94, 95
Benvorlich, S.S. : 21
Boggs, Captain L. S. : 146
Bonnieville, S.S. : 110
Brilliant, U.S.S. : 45
British Sailors' Society : 15, 112
British War Relief Society of the U.S.A. : 15

Brook, Commodore J., R.N.R. : 49
Broughton, Surgeon Lieutenant W. D., R.N.V.R. : 133
Brown, Captain L. E. : 35, 36, 41-44, 129, 156
Bruce, S.S. : 108
Bury. S.S. 35, 36 41-44, 129-13
also Pic. Betwben 76-77.

C

Campbell, Captain G. L. : 105
Campfire, S.S. : 91
Canadian Red Cross : 16, 112
Carras, S.S. : 117
Celtic Star, S.S. : 104
Charles L. D., S.S. : 51
Chelmer, H.M.S. : 144
Christopher Newport, S.S. : 57, 67
Churchill, Winston S. : 160
City of Waterford, S.S. : 26
Clarke, Captain G. L. : 27
Clyde Shipping Company : 18, 54 135
Coastal Command of the R.A.F. : 145
Cochrane, H.M.S. : xii
Cocle, S.S. : 35
Convoy Medical Code : 166-7 (Appendix III)
Convoys *ONS 92* : 35, *ONS C 122* : 37, *P Q 17* : 53-69, 79, 92, *QP 14* : 84, 90, 96, *PQ 18* : 84-92, *RA 60* : 98, *SC 118* : 103, *ONS 7* : 114, *ON 151* : 115, *SC 121* : 116, *SC 122* : 116, *KMS 23* : 131, *ONS 18* : 132, 133, *ON 202* : 132, *ONS 27* : 139, *ON 218* : 139, *ON 225* : 142, *SC 156* : 143, *ONC 260* : 148
Cossack, H.M.S. : 49.
Cyrus H. McCormick, S.S. : 152, 153

D

Dalcroy, S.S. : 45
Dartford, S.S. : 36, 37
Dawson, Chief Engineer A. S. : 62, 64, 67
Deptford, H.M.S. : 28
Denison, Commodore, E. C., R.N.R. : 154
Deveron, H.M.S. : 140, 141
Dove, Captain P. : 49
Dowding, Commodore, J. C. K., R.N.R. : 65, 67, 69, 70, 94
Dunbar-Nasmith, Admiral Sir Martin : 6
Dundee, Perth, and London Shipping Company : 124, 135

E

Earnshaw, Chief Officer H. K. : 46
Eedanger, M.V. : 34
Eimerl, Surgeon Lieutenant T. S., R.N.V.R. : 152
Elderton, Sir William : xix
Empire Antelope, S.S. : 46
Empire Beaumont, S.S. : 87, 88
Empire Dell, S.S. : 35
Empire Gold, S.S. : 152
Empire Heritage, S.S. : 146, 148
Empire Leopard, S.S. : 46
Empire McColl, S.S. : 127
Empire MacGadila, S.S. : 127
Empire Mersey, S.S. : 40
Empire Moat, S.S. : 26
Empire Sunrise, S.S. : 45
Empire Tide, S.S. : 72, 74
Empire Union, S.S. : 101
Empire Wave, S.S. : 5

F

Fea, Captain T. E. : 37, 47
Fort Cedar Lake, S.S. : 117
Franckel, Commander, U.S.N. : 70, **73**
Frederick Douglas, S.S. : 132, 133

G

General Steam Navigation Company : 135
Geneva Conventions : 25, 159
Glass, Captain G. N. : 131-135, 156
Glennie, Surgeon Lieutenant, R.N.V.R. : 104
Golovko, Admiral Arseni, Soviet Navy : 55, 92
Good, Captain R. : 108, 109
Goodwin, Captain, R.A.M.C. : 75
Gray Ranger, R.F.A. : 94, 95
Greenham, Captain A. W. R. M. : 106, 107
Gretton, Vice-Admiral Sir Peter : 119

H

Haddon, Captain J. M. : 37, 39, 128, 152
Hague Convention 1907 : 1, 157
Hahoia, S.S. : 47
Halifax, Nova Scotia : 10, 16, 44, 103
Harris, Captain J. : 124-128, 140, 141, 156
Hartley, Captain W. G. : 85, 114, 143, 156
Harvester, H.M.S. : 116
Hatasu, S.S. : 5
Hatcher, Captain W. H. : 119
HF/DF : 25, 158
Hill, Rear-Admiral R. A. S. : 9
Holmes, Surgeon Lieutenant P. N., R.N.V.R. : 146, 147
Horton, Admiral Sir Max : xiii, 136, 150, 154, 160
Hospital Ships : 157
Hudson, Captain G. K. : 19, 100-105.
Hughes, Chief Officer W. : 125, 126

I

Intourist Hotel : 77
Inverader, S.S. : 34

J

J. van Rensselaer, S.S. : 107
Joel R. Poinsett, S.S. : 142

K

Kaiser, H. : 106
Kanin Noss : 84
Kara Sea : 71
Katvaldis, S.S. : 37
Kelly, Surgeon Lieutenant,
   R.N.V.R. : 49
Kentucky, S.S. : 91
King Edward, S.S. : 101
King Gruffyd, S.S. : 117
Kingsbury, S.S. : 117, 118
Kirnwood, S.S. : 29
Knell, Captain A. J. : 34

L

Laidler, Captain W. : 118
La Malouine, F.F.S. : 93
Lawford, Captain E. D. W., R.N. :
   68
Leda, H.M.S. : 94
Linon, Docteur Henri : 163
Lissa, Battle of : 1.
Llanover, S.S. : 35
Longfield, Mate M. G. : 63
Lotus, H.M.S. : 65
Low, Chief Engineer A. B. : 111

M

MacBain, Surgeon Lieutenant G.,
   R.N.V.R. : 59, 63, 64, 73, 74,
   81, 82
Malantic, S.S. : 108, 109;
Mallory, U.S.S. : 105
Martin, H.M.S. : 90
Mary Luchenback, S.S. : 89
Matochkin Strait : 66
Maunde, Captain G., R.N. : 70,
   73
McAddie, Chief Engineer D. : 40,
   152

McCallum, Surgeon Lieutenant
   W. H., R.N.V.R. : 64, 81, 82, 93
McGowan, Captain C. K. : 53, 54,
   58, 59, 96, 102
McKellar, Captain J. : 84, 138,
   139, 156
McNee, Sir John, Surgeon Rear-
   Admiral, Consulting Physician
   to the Royal Navy in Scotland :
   113, 123, 136
McPherson, Chief Engineer W. :
   85
McRae, Second Officer R. : 131,
   156
Melrose Abbey, S.S. : 101
Merchant Ship Aircraft Carriers
   (MAC) : 121
Miller, Chief Engineer W. McD. :
   62, 67
Ministry of War Transport : 4, 13,
   15, 24, 25, 32, 36, 144, 151
Moffat, Boatswain W. : 115
Moller Bay : 71
Morison, Rear - Admiral S. E.,
   U.S.N. : 119
Morris, Captain Owen C. : 20,
   53, 54, 83, 96, 115, 117, 118
Moss, Surgeon Lieutenant S. D.,
   R.N.V.R. : 112
Mount Taurus, S.S. : 48
Moville : 145
Murmansk : 55, 79, 80
Murphy, H. C. : 113
Murray, Captain J. : 148-150

N

Nailsea, S.S. : 110
Nationality of Survivors : 164,
   Appendix I
Nikolins Matkovic, S.S. : 39
Noble, Admiral Sir Percy, xiii
Northern Gem, H.M.T. : 94
Northern Wave, H.M.T. : 115,
   147
North of Scotland, Orkney, and
   Shetlands Steamship Company :
   102

O

Ocean Freedom, S.S. : 62
Ocean Voice, S.S. : 94
Oldham, S.S. : 145
Oliver Elsworth, S.S. : 86
Olympus, S.S. : 19
Outram, Reverend F. H.,
   R.N.V.R. : 77

P

Palomares, H.M.S. : 55, 65
Parismina, S.S. : 48
Parthenon, S.S. : 46, 47
Paulus Potter, S.S. : 93
Perth and London Shipping Com-
   pany : 21
Pozarika, H.M.S. : 55, 68
President Sergeant, S.S. : 48

R

Reed, J. A., Asst Secretary, U.S.
   Treasury : 161
Rescue Ships—Convoys Escorted
   and Survivors Rescued . 165,
   Appendix II
   Aboyne : 124-128, 139-141
   Accrington : 32, 106
   Bury : 29, 32, 35, 36, 41, 129,
      130
   Copeland : 18, 84-92, 96-98,
      114, 115, 143
   Dewsbury : 29, 30, 32, 33
   Dundee : 135, 136, 148-150
   Eddystone : 135, 142, 143
   Empire Comfort : 151
   Empire Lifeguard : 151
   Empire Peacemaker : 151
   Empire Rest : 151
   Empire Shelter : 151
   Fastnet : 138, 139
   Goodwin : 105, 113, 114, 123,
      143
   Gothland : 32, 36, 38, 40, 41,
      128, 152, 153
   Hontestroom : 17, 18, 26

   Melrose Abbey : 23, 108-110
   Perth : 21-23, 48-50
   Pinto : 135, 136, 146-148, 150
   Rathlin : 29, 32, 53, 92-95, 98,
      100, 131-134
   St Clair : 138
   Stockport : 29, 32, 37, 45-48,
      105, 114
   St Sunniva : 102, 103, 106, 114
   Syrian Prince : 135
   Tjaldur : 29
   Toward : 18, 34, 100, 101, 103-
      105, 114
   Walmer Castle : 26
   Zaafaran : 19, 20, 53-64, 101,
      102, 114
   Zamalek : 19, 20, 31, 53-69,
      92-95, 98, 115-119, 155
River Afton, S.S. : 65
Rose, H.M.S. : 50
Rosenberg, S.S. : 113
Royal National Life-boat Institu-
   tion : 162, 163
Rudland, Surgeon Commander
   R. S., R.N.V.R. : xiii
Ruth, S.S. : 144

S

Salamander, H.M.S. : 62
Samuel Chase, S.S. : 94
Scharnhorst, Ger. battle cruiser :
   99
Seagull, H.M.T. : 94
Sea Transport, Director of : 7, 17
Sevroles Hospital : 76, 78
Seydisfiord . 95
Sheaf Mount, S.S. : 37
Shearer, Captain A. H. : 156
Shipping, Ministry of : 7
Silver Sword, S.S. : 94
Smith, Surgeon Lieutenant A. W.,
   R.N.V.R. : 150
Snowden, Captain A. J. E. : 29,
   33, 156
Soekaboeni, S.S. : 101
Somali, H.M.S. : 94
South America, M.V. : 143, 144

Southern Empress, S.S. : 39
Spartiate, H.M.S. : xii
Steel Voyager, S.S. : 134
Susana, S.S. : 39
Swale, H.M.S. : 144

U.S. Coastguard Service : 161
U.S. Maritime Administration : 44
U.S. Navy Department : 106
U.S. Naval Institute Proceedings : 161

T

Texas Oil Company : 144
Theodore Dwight Weld, S.S. : 132, 133
Theodore Parker, S.S. : 139-141
Thomson, Chief Engineer A. W. : 148
Tirpitz, Ger. battleship : 52, 58, 99
Tolken, S.S. : 36
Trade Division of the Admiralty : 7, 24
Troup, Vice-Admiral Sir James : xii, xiii
Tuscaloosa, U.S.S. : 79, 80

V

Vian, Admiral of the Fleet, Sir Philip : 49
Viscount, H.M.S. : 38

W

Warfield, S.S. : 131
White Sea : 84
Wilkins, Surgeon Lieutenant R. D., R.N.V.R. : 56, 70-73, 78, 81, 95, 156
William Hooper, S.S. : 57, 58
Williamson, Captain K. : 48, 50
Winston Salem, S.S. : 70-73
Wolf, Chief Radio Officer C. : 73, 82, 103

U

U-boats : 34, 38, 45, 99, 104, 134, *U-302:* 144